SKITS THAT TEACH
VOLUME 2

EDDIE JAMES AND TOMMY WOODARD
THE SKIT GUYS

BANNED IN WISCONSIN
35 CHEESE-FREE SKITS

D1709719

youth specialties

ZONDERVAN.com/
AUTHORTRACKER
follow your favorite authors

ZONDERVAN

Skits That Teach, Volume 2
Copyright © 2011 by Eddie James and Tommy Woodard

YS Youth Specialties is a trademark of YOUTHWORKS!, INCORPORATED and is registered with the United States Patent and Trademark Office.

This title is also available as a Zondervan ebook.
Visit www.zondervan.com/ebooks.

This title is also available in a Zondervan audio edition.
Visit www.zondervan.fm.

Requests for information should be addressed to:

Zondervan, *Grand Rapids, Michigan 49530*

Library of Congress Cataloging-in-Publication Data

James, Eddie, 1970–
    Skits that teach, Volume 2 / by Eddie James and Tommy Woodard.
       p.   cm.
    Includes bibliographical references and index.
    ISBN 978-0-310-89199-X (softcover : alk. paper) 1. Drama in Christian education. 2. Church group work with teenagers. 3. Christian drama, American. 4. One-act plays, American. I. Woodard, Tommy. II. Title. III. Title: Skits that teach, volume two. IV. Title: Skits that teach.
    BV1534.4.J3425 2012
    268'.67—dc23   2011030699

Cover design: SharpSeven Design
Interior design: David Conn

Printed in the United States of America

11 12 13 14 15 16 /PHP/ 23 22 21 20 19 18 17 16 15 14 13 12 11 10 9 8 7 6 5 4 3 2 1

DEDICATION

To the four greatest kids in the world who allow their dads to act like geeks onstage. (And you still call us "father" without any embarrassment...or at least you don't tell us...)

Abby Woodard

Hudson Woodard

Ainsley James

Jayci James

ACKNOWLEDGMENTS

We want to thank our wives, Angie and Stephanie. If they hadn't said yes to this life we live, we wouldn't be doing it. Our families come first, and we are thankful they let us do what we get to do as a "job."

"Wow Factor" to Monty Priest and Gary Singleton, our pastors, who still trust us to perform for the congregations we're a part of (and who still see the big picture).

Doug Fields for still mentoring both of us.

Brian Cates, Jay Howver, Tim Antone, Rian Slay, David Rogers, Jonathan Matlock, and Sarah Wall for being the best staff we could ask for.

Special thanks to all of our authors at www.skitguys.com—Rob Courtney, Brian Cropp, Tami Duncan, GinnyLee Ellis, Ben Gazaway, Chris Hurt, Ted and Nancie Lowe, Knox McCoy, Rian Slay, Sarah Vanderaa, Carrie Varnell, Sarah Wall, Melinda Whitten, and Rebecca Wimmer. You've made this book what it is, and we are honored to do life with you!

Huge handfuls of glitter thrown in the air for Carrie Varnell and Charissa Fishbeck: All the time that went into this book was made simpler because of your help and diligence in filtering through the scripts, editing, rewording, and "red-flagging"—we have a great book on our hands!

PREFACE

We've been blown away by the success of *Skits That Teach*. So many students and adults have used that book to help them in their churches, banquets, dinner theaters, and even mission trips.

One key difference you'll notice in *Skits That Teach, Volume Two* is that in addition to our own contributions, we've enlisted the talents of some incredibly gifted writers with different takes on life, comedy, and those dramatic moments. Once we published the first book, we came in contact with some very funny and creative people from around the nation who are also using their gifts and talents for God. So instead of trying to reinvent the wheel of our own Christian skit scripts, we thought we'd approach it from a totally different perspective with these great writers. They've all become our good friends, and we consider them part of our Skit Guys family. And please know that we—Eddie and Tommy—not only read and approved each script submitted by our writer friends, but in many cases we reworked or made some adjustments to them so they'd carry that Skit Guys "flavor." (Much like Five Guys burgers without the trans-fat!)

And by the way, if you read these scripts and say to yourself, *I write skits like this, too!* then what are you waiting for? Jump on www.skitguys.com to find out how to submit at least five scripts, and maybe you can be part of the Skit Guys family, too.

Throughout this book we also mention a DVD called *Skit Training 101*. Everywhere we go, to our constant amazement and gratification, we field questions about how to start, maintain, or improve a drama team. This DVD contains all of our "secrets," and we would be remiss not to recommend it. You may have an acting team full of drama, but that doesn't mean you have a great drama team! Whether you're leading a team of student or adult actors, the *Skit Training 101* interactive DVD-ROM gives you everything you need to create comedy and drama that engages, entertains, and educates. We become your "drama coaches in a box," so to speak.

The DVD will show you how to—

* start a drama team and equip the members to "run with it,"
* write your own scripts,
* improve previously published scripts,
* memorize scripts with ease (like the ones in this book),
* coach your actors,

…and much, much more.

Your talent is a gift from God.
What you do with that talent is your gift back to God.
We hope you have as much fun reading and using this book as we had putting it together.
Blessings as you act, write, and direct,

Tommy Woodard and Eddie James
The Skit Guys

CONTENTS

INTRODUCTION

0.0

HERE WE GO AGAIN!

More than five years ago, we set out to answer the question, "What's wrong with Christian skits today?" The answers were numerous, ranging from "They're too cheesy" to "They're repetitive" to "They're not funny" to "They're repetitive." (Get it?)

In *Skits That Teach*, we attempted to create Christian-themed scripts that lacked the deficits of most skits in Christendom. We received responses such as:

> "Finally a skit book I am not ashamed to give to my drama team."
> "Thank you, thank you, thank you for a book that has great skits and solid content!"
> "Fall-down-laughing skit material that is Scripture-filled but not too preachy."
> "One of the funniest books I've ever read."
> "The best skit material on the market."
> "We love these skits! They are thought-provoking and not at all goofy."
> "This transformed my abs in only 90 days!"

(Okay, that last one is from the P90X® commercial...but a good laugh *can* be a decent ab workout!)

We received several requests for a second volume of *Skits That Teach*—which is what you have in your hands right now. We followed the same mission we had many years ago: Provide "lactose-free" Christian scripts for your youth group or drama team. Our hope is that we've created a follow-up like *The Empire Strikes Back*, rather than *The Temple of Doom*. (You know...a *good* sequel!)

As we did in the first volume, let's take a few minutes to cover the crucial elements to creating the best skits possible. We've even added a few more to round out some problem areas. This is what we call **THE TOP-10 NUTS AND BOLTS OF CREATING THE BEST SKITS POSSIBLE!** (Eh...maybe we'll work on that title later. Anyway...)

1. **Cut the Cheese.** We've tried to make sure these skits are suitable for the lactose intolerant. To be more accurate, we're claiming that these skits are 98% cheese-free! However, what we believe is cheese-less, you may believe is chock-full of cheddar. So if it's cheesy to you, then by all means, change it!

2. **No Groovy Dialogue.** Believe it or not, it's easy for a pair of fortysomething dudes to write dialogue that eventually becomes dated. So we've done our best to avoid phrases, sayings, and clichés that will make you sound totally gnarly and drastically affect your coolness factor. (Again, we encourage you to change anything that doesn't sound right to you. That way you can keep it real and people will think you're the "cat's meow.")

3. **Don't Quote Me on This.** Although these scripts contain biblical truth, we promise you'll never hear one of our characters say, "The Bible says…" In fact many times your audience will learn what the Bible says without even knowing it came from the Bible.

4. **The Names Have Been Changed to Protect the Innocent.** You may not like the characters' names and want to change them—great! Do it. Just don't use *your* name. There's nothing more counterproductive than watching a skit or a scene in which a character uses the actor's real name. Please let the audience see you as someone *different*.

5. **Funny Is in the Eye of the Beholder.** Have you ever told a hilarious joke only to have the person to whom you told the joke smile, give you a courtesy laugh, and say, "I don't get it"? We have too, and we hate the way that feels. So hear us when we say that we believe what we've written for you here is pretty darn funny! On top of that, most of these skits have already passed inspection, as they've been performed all across the nation and in front of diverse audiences—and everyone laughed. (Okay, not everyone. But the people who didn't laugh were mean…and unintelligent…and no one really likes them anyway.)

6. **He Stinketh.** There's nothing worse than stinking—whether it's due to a crummy performance or the chalupa you ate for lunch. Nobody likes to walk away from a skit while struggling to look people in the eye as they say things like: "Hey, you guys are getting better!" or "Sure looks like you all are working real hard at that drama stuff!" or "Wow! That was amazingly horrible. I mean, that sucker really stank. I think you guys just set a new world's record for the longest stinky skit ever performed." (Seriously, our youth pastor uttered that last one when we were younger. It still stings!) We can't promise your skits won't stink. What we *can* promise is that we've done all we can to try to keep them fresh and odor-free. Your job is to make sure your actors are prepared before they walk onstage. No matter how big your audience, if a skit is worth doing, it's worth doing to the best of your ability.

7. **Theology Schmeeology.** Think this one's about our theological beliefs? A discussion of the book of Revelation, perhaps? Nope. It's about *predictability*! Just as we bucked your predictions or expectations here, we've made a great effort to do that with these skits. Many of them don't have the happy ending where everyone

comes to Jesus and pantomimes a sing-along tune. Sometimes you may even see a main character make the wrong decision and suffer for it. Our goal isn't to wrap up everything with a neat little bow; we'd rather you engage your audience and let them think and wrestle with issues. We want you to hear your audience say, "I didn't see that coming!"

8. **Create a Studio.** Work at having not only actors, but also a couple of directors, writers, and even props. If you do, you'll notice your drama team getting bigger just because not everyone is ON the stage—the people OFF stage are making the skits, the scripts, the blocking, and the visuals all better because you have a full "studio" pulling off this slice of life. (*Skit Training 101* goes into more depth regarding how to pull this off. If you're interested. We're not trying to be car salesmen.)

9. **Red Ink and Improv.** When working through the script, invest in some red ink pens. Circle stuff that doesn't sound the way your town, culture, or part of the universe would speak. Maybe one of your writers (from your studio!) thought of something better or funnier to say. Circle the "red flags" and talk about what changes to make. Improv your new verbiage and see what fits. Just keep the MESSAGE intact.

10. **A Good Friend Told Us.** When we started out doing the skit thing in high school, we took along a friend of ours named Chris Jones. He was a great encourager and helper as we traveled. He always said, "Pretend like Jesus is in the front row laughing, crying, smiling—enjoying the performance." Chris' words have stuck with us. What we're doing onstage—in God's name—should honor God, honor Scripture, and honor the world we live in. It also should be challenging, comedic, sentimental, and enjoyable.

11. **You Have the Hardest Job.** (Okay, this isn't really a Top-10 List!) Performing Christian skits is probably the hardest thing you'll do when it comes to "the stage." Audiences who gather to witness plays, musicals, dinner theatre shows, improv—they're all ready for something "good." But typical audiences for Christian skits are just ready to get it over with. They're expecting "cheesy" and thinking, *Oh, there's the Jesus part* or *How many times can they put hell into a four-minute skit?* Be different, friends! Rise above the mediocrity and create great skits, be great actors—blow your audiences' minds and hearts and souls regarding what Christian skits can be. It's up to you…now go get 'em!

We still believe that "humor breaks down walls for truth to enter." It's a proven fact: If you can make an audience laugh, that audience will listen to you. So earn the right to be heard.

Eddie & Tommy
The Skit Guys

P.S. If at some point you can't seem to find that perfect script for your group, please come see us at www.skitguys.com where we have hundreds of scripts and videos to help you out.

SKITS FOR IDIOTS

INTRO

Idiot Is a Term of Endearment

Okay, it really isn't a term of endearment. However, we do mean it in a positive sense. As in, *These skits are easier to pull off than the other skits in this book—so easy, in fact, that even an idiot could perform them.* We *were* going to call this chapter "So Easy That a Monkey Could Perform It," but we'd rather offend your actors than all the primates in the world!

Just because a skit is easy, that doesn't mean it isn't good. Take eating half a dozen doughnuts, for example—*easy* and *good*! This collection of scripts also may be the most eclectic in the book. There's comedy, drama, and some are both. And the subject matter covers everything from faith, to kids, to robbery!

In the end you'll find these skits have good messages and are easy to put together—with minimal prop requirements and simple staging. In most cases there are very few lines to memorize; in some cases the actors can even hold their scripts during the performance. (We weren't kidding when we said these were written for idiots!)

For more help, check out the "Page Down" method found in *Skit Training 101* to help your idiots—umm, we mean *actors*—memorize their scripts.

Skit Tips

Just because these are simple skits, that doesn't mean you don't have to put in a little effort. Here are some ideas to keep in mind as you prepare to use "Skits for Idiots":

1. **Read through the script in advance.** This will help you secure the actors you'll need to play each role and give you time to pull together the necessary props.

2. **Choose actors who can improv.** As with any performance, mistakes are a possibility. So your actors need to "roll with the punches." But that possibility is intensified when a skit is thrown together just a few minutes before the performance. So be sure your "idiots" are flexible!

3. **Make each script your own.** Make all of the changes you want to make to the script *before* you give copies of it to your actors. You should feel free to cut or rewrite portions of the script to make it easier for your actors or to make it work with an accompanying message.

4. **Have fun!** Above all, have a great time with these scripts. Use them as tools to praise your drama team. And if you tell the audience that the actors received their scripts just 30 minutes before performance time, they'll look like master thespians! (Of course, then we'll have to change the name of this chapter...)

"ALL GROWED UP"

BY CHRIS HURT, WITH REVISIONS BY TOMMY WOODARD AND EDDIE JAMES

WHAT: Two kindergarteners demonstrate their love of Jesus and their confusion with the way adults interpret the same relationship.

WHO: Ryan, Chad, Ms. Johnson (Sunday school teacher)

WHEN: Present Day

WHY: Matthew 19:14-15; Luke 18:15-17; Galatians 3:26

WEAR:
(COSTUMES AND PROPS) Bible, plastic toy lion

HOW: Trust the script to bring out childlike qualities in the actors, rather than the actors using "baby talk." However, the more invested the actors are in the young characters, the funnier the skit will be.

THEMES: Childlike Faith, Loving Jesus, Church Attendance, Relationship Versus Religion

TIME: 5 to 6 minutes

The scene opens on a kindergarten Sunday school class.

Teacher: All right, class. Everyone settle down. For those of you who are new this week, I'm Ms. Johnson. Sunday school will begin in just a few minutes. I need to get some more pipe cleaners and macaroni for our craft, but I'll be right back. You boys behave yourself. Chad, you're in charge.

Chad: Did you hear that? I'm in charge. I'm in charge. So you gotta do what I say.

Ryan: That's not fair. I'm not gonna do what you say.

Chad: You better. I'm in charge.

Ryan:	Uh *uh.*
Chad:	Uh *huh.*
Ryan:	Uh *uh.*
Chad:	Uh *huh.*
Ryan:	Uh *uh.*
Chad:	I am TOO! Ms. Johnson SAID I was! *(Yells offstage)* Ms. Johnson, Ryan is *not* submitting to my authority!
Ryan:	You're dumb.
Chad:	So?
Ryan:	You gonna get another gold star?
Chad:	Yep. I'm gonna get another gold star 'cuz I've been to church every Sunday, and I have memorized all of my Bible verses. I got a whole *bunch* of gold stars. And if I get five more stars, I get some ice cream. Ice cream…I love ice cream. I scream, you scream, we all scream for ice cream… *(Stops abruptly and starts picking his nose)*
Ryan:	What are you doing?
Chad:	Getting a booger. *(Looks for place to wipe the booger)*
Ryan:	Gross…you are so gross.
Chad:	Am not.
Ryan:	Are too.
Chad:	Am not.
Ryan:	Are too.
Chad:	Ooooh…look! A Bible!
Ryan:	That's mine.
Chad:	Finders keepers, losers weepers!

Ryan:	Fine, I'll trade ya.
Chad:	Ooooh, okay!
Ryan:	Oh, man. *(Trades him for a plastic toy lion)*
Chad:	I love the missionaries that came to class last week.
Ryan:	Me too.
Chad:	I especially like the super-cool leprosy pictures.
Ryan:	Ooooooh, I couldn't eat pizza for a week.
Chad:	I wanna be a missionary when I grow up.
Ryan:	Where ya gonna be a missionary?
Chad:	Africa…
Ryan:	Africa. That's awesome. I hope you don't get eaten by lions or anything.
Chad:	*(Looking at lion toy)* Yeah, me too. Here comes Ms. Johnson. Everybody quiet!
Teacher:	Okay guys, looks like there are no pipe cleaners or macaroni in this church. Let's do something else. How many of you memorized this week's verse?
Ryan:	Oooh! Ooooh…me, me! Okay, "God is love."
Chad:	Oooh! Ooooh…I know a verse…"Jesus wept."
Teacher:	Okay, okay, those are both good verses. Good job, boys.
Chad:	Can we sing a song, Ms. Johnson?
Both:	Yes, a song…please, please… "Lord's Army," "Jesus Loves Me"… *(Name several popular children's songs)*

Both *start singing a popular children's worship or praise song.*

Teacher:	Beautiful, beautiful. So what do you guys want to be when you grow up?

Chad:	A firefighter, and I'll put out all kinds of fires. No wait, a cop, oh, wait—the President—ooh, I'll be the next *(Name a popular TV personality)*, and I'll run every show on late night, AND I'll be the best missionary you ever saw.
Ryan:	I want to clean swimming pools.
Teacher:	Okay, I guess cleanliness *is* next to godliness. Let's all say John 3:16.
Both:	*(Chanting)* John three-sixteen!
Teacher:	Oh, boy…okay…tell me something about Jesus. *(Teacher looks around at "other" students and then chooses Chad who's raising his hand frantically)*
Chad:	Jesus was a man who lived a long time ago, and he rode in a sled with a reindeer, and he wears red and has a beard.
Ryan:	No, that's Satan. Jesus had a brown beard, and he wore sandals. And he held lambs a lot. And he has a halo over his head…and he always looked like this. *(Makes classic Jesus portrait pose, including morose facial expression)*
Teacher:	Oh, look at the time! It's time to head to worship, thank goodness! Don't forget to memorize your verse for next week, and oh, bring a friend…I guess. See you guys next week!
Chad:	So much for Sunday school.
Ryan:	I like Sunday school, but I wish we could take Jesus home with us every day.
Chad:	Yeah, but I love coming to church and visiting Jesus.
Ryan:	Me too. I come to church every Sunday with my mom and dad, and we talk to Jesus here. *(Pause)* But we don't talk to Jesus much at home.
Chad:	Me neither.
Ryan:	Yeah. How can I memorize Bible verses when Mommy and Daddy don't?
Chad:	Yeah, I know. Maybe we're supposed to talk to Jesus only on Sundays at church.

Ryan:	Like our parents do.
Chad:	I wish we could take Jesus home with us.
Ryan:	Yeah, if I was all growed up, I'd take Jesus home with me and spend time with him all week long.
Chad:	Yeah…me too.
Both:	*(As they exit)* Bye, Jesus. See you next week.

THE END

SKIT 1.2

"ATTEMPTED ROBBERY"
BY CHRIS HURT

WHAT: The Devil boldly confronts a believer in this skit, but the believer is more than ready for the confrontation.

WHO: T. L., Satan

WHEN: Present Day

WHY: John 10:10; Romans 16:19-20; 1 Peter 5:8-9

WEAR: A newspaper, a hat for Satan to wear
(COSTUMES AND PROPS)

HOW: Although the subject matter is Satan and temptation, keep a light tone and a fast pace.

THEMES: Satan, Spiritual Warfare, Temptation, Authority

TIME: 6 to 7 minutes

As the scene opens, **T. L.** *is reading the newspaper.* **Satan** *enters.*

Satan: Stick 'em up.

T. L.: I'm sorry?

Satan: Stick 'em up. I've got a gun, and I'm not afraid to use it.

T. L.: Okay, okay…they're up.

Satan: Put the paper down. *(T. L. lowers the paper and therefore his hands)* Keep your hands up. *(T. L. raises hands, therefore raising the paper again)* Put the paper down. Keep the paper down.

T. L.: But you said…

Satan:	Put the paper down. Keep your hands up. *(Takes the paper and throws it down)*
T. L.:	But you said…
Satan:	Forget what I said…now hand it over.
T. L.:	I'm sorry. I'm not sure what you want me to hand over, but…is that your finger?
Satan:	Yes!
T. L.:	You're using your finger as a gun? You are actually using your *finger* as a gun. This is ridiculous! Excuse me, I have some reading to do, so if you don't mind… *(Moves to pick up the newspaper)*
Satan:	*(Looking at his finger)* In hell all guns look like this, so now who feels like an idiot? Hmm?
T. L.:	Okay, this is ridiculous. Please leave. I get it—you're all freaky and stuff. I'm super scared. So can you please take the freak show to the next town?
Satan:	You still don't know who I am, do you?
T. L.:	I have no idea, and here's something—I don't care to know. So it was a real pleasure meeting you, have a good day, and I hope to see you soon.
Satan:	It was nice to meet you too, actually. Hey, why do they call you "T. L."? What does it stand for?
T. L.:	Terence Lamar. Wait, how did you know my name is T. L.?

In answer, **Satan** *starts making stereotypical "devil" noises and dancing around* **T. L.** *while hissing and making "scary" faces.*

T. L.:	Well, I'm almost afraid to ask, but what are you doing?
Satan:	Shhh…I'm the Prince of Darkness…just go with it…
T. L.:	The prince of…?
Satan:	I'm the Father of Lies.

T. L.:	Are you that weird uncle I've never met? Uncle Palford, is that you?
Satan:	Aren't you horrified by me?
T. L.:	No.
Satan:	I'm Beelzebub…Little Horn…the Tempter…Dragon…
T. L.:	Okay, I'm sorry. Are these nicknames? I don't really…
Satan:	*(Drops his "scary" act)* Come on, man. It's me, Satan. Satan! The Red One. The Keeper of Hell.
T. L.:	Funny, I thought you'd be taller. Okay, Satan, nice to meet you. Do I call you Satan or the Devil or Mr. Devil? Maybe Beelzebub or just plain "Bub"?
Satan:	Mr. Devil is just fine.
T. L.:	Okay, Mr. Devil? Let me ask you some questions. Where are your horns?
Satan:	Under my hat.
T. L.:	Do you own a trident? You know…that three-pronged pitchfork?
Satan:	That's a myth. I'm the Devil, not Poseidon.
T. L.:	Is hell really hot?
Satan:	So hot that the chickens lay fried eggs.
T. L.:	Wow, really?
Satan:	Yes, and it's totally annoying since the missus has cut out all fried foods from my diet.
T. L.:	And you really went down to Georgia?
Satan:	Yes, I was looking for a soul to steal. I was in a bind, I was way behind, I was willing to make a deal. *(Under his breath)* Stupid Johnny!
T. L.:	Okay, this is ridiculous. All right, Mr. Satan, what do you want?
Satan:	I'm going to rise up from the pits of darkness to wreak havoc, despair, gloom, and tragedy into your life. There will be torment, catastrophe,

hurricanes, windstorms, and a whole plethora of stuff you can't even fathom.

T. L.:   Huh?

Satan: Basically, I came here to steal, kill, and destroy. In a nutshell. Lots of stealing, killing, and destroying. And it starts NOW.

T. L.:   Okay, now?

Satan: Now.

T. L.:   Has it started?

Satan: Now.

T. L.:   Now. So...now?

Satan: NOW.

T. L.:   Okay. I don't feel any different.

Satan: *(Awkward pause)* Now. Give me an inch, and I'll be your ruler.

T. L.:   Gotcha. Listen, I really need to get some reading done now, so what did you say you came here to do? Were you going to steal something?

Satan: I was going to steal your joy. That's what I do. I steal joy! I take your joy, and I steal it. Here's Joy: *(High voice)* "Oh, I am so glad to see you." Here's me: *(Deep voice)* "Joy, you're coming with me. You're totally mine now." Here's Joy: *(High voice)* "No, you can't. I'm so happy all the time. Just happy, happy, happy." Here's me: *(Deep voice)* "Joy, I'm going to steal you, and then I'm going to pound your face in. I don't like you, Joy, so now you're mine, and I will beat you senseless. Take that, Joy. You like that, Joy?" *(Mimes beating someone up)*

T. L.:   Mr. Devil...wow...are you okay? Listen, you can't have my joy. You see, the joy I have doesn't belong to me. It's a gift. So it's not really mine for you to steal.

Satan: Well, too bad. You won't notice that I'm stealing it because I'll be too busy killing. I'll kill your purpose—that's what I'll kill. You won't even have a reason to live.

T. L.:	You can't kill my purpose. I don't live for myself.
Satan:	That doesn't make sense. I'm going to steal, kill, and I'm going to destroy. Why, you ask? Because I'm a roaring lion, and I'm looking for someone to devour. Roar…
T. L.:	Are you a lion? Or are you a-lyin'? Get it? Are you a *lion*—like the Cowardly Lion—or are you "a-lyin'," as in not telling me the truth?
Satan:	You know what? That's not funny, and it kinda hurts when you make fun of me. And yes, I will destroy…
T. L.:	Can't.
Satan:	I will destroy…
T. L.:	Can't.
Satan:	Can!
T. L.:	Can't.
Satan:	Can!
T. L.:	Can't.
Satan:	Why?
T. L.:	I'll tell you why, all right? Because I'm really growing tired of you. Here it is: You can't mess with me because I belong to Jesus. You hear that? I belong to the King of Kings.
Satan:	I'm sorry?
T. L.:	Jesus.
Satan:	Noooooooooooo! *(Cowers on the floor)* I don't like that. I don't like that Jesus. I don't like him.
T. L.:	So here's the deal. I'm dead to sin. Sin has no power over me. I belong to Christ, and therefore, you have no power over me. You can try to tempt me. You can try to steal, kill, and destroy. But the bottom line is this: You have no power here. I am free because the Son has set me free indeed.

Satan: *(Gives up)* Well, it was a pleasure meeting you. Maybe we can get together another time?

T. L.: *(Almost interrupting)* No, no, not going to happen.

Satan: Okay, well, I'm off to wreak havoc and advise several world leaders. Wish me luck!

T. L.: Good luck. *(Starts to walk off)* Actually, I don't really believe in luck, nor do I want to see you do well. However, I do believe in the Word of God and that your fate has been determined—and it ain't pretty. So good luck…with THAT.

THE END

"FAITH FOR SALE"

BY BRIAN CROPP, WITH REVISIONS BY TOMMY WOODARD AND EDDIE JAMES

WHAT: With all of the religions in the world, how can we know for sure that there's just one way to heaven?

WHO: Jack, Vendor, Mary

WHEN: Present Day

WHY: John 14:6; 1 John 5:11-13

WEAR: Vendor booth, small ceramic doll, necklace, Zen sand garden, Bonsai tree,
(COSTUMES AND PROPS) rosary beads, prayer shawl, WWJD? bracelet, napkin, map

HOW: Due to the lack of resolution to this skit, it would be best used as a discussion starter. Put a lot of energy into each character, and the audience will laugh along with you.

THEMES: Faith, Religion, Assurance, Confusion

TIME: 5 to 7 minutes

---

*The setting is a city street. A street **Vendor** waits for customers. **Jack** and **Mary**, who are on vacation, enter the stage.*

Mary: *(Examining a map)* Okay, well I think, according to this, if we can catch the train at 131st Street, we can make it to the museum in plenty of time to…

Jack: Are we going to have time to…

Mary: Yes, that's what I'm telling you.

Vendor: *(In a foreign accent)* Excuse me. Would I be correct in thinking that you are new to the area?

Mary: Actually, we are on our vacation.

Jack *pulls* **Mary** *aside.*

Jack: *(Under his breath)* Don't tell him that. That's how people get mugged.

Mary: Please, Jack, it's not like we're on an episode of *CSI*.

Vendor: No, Miss, your husband is right. You cannot be too careful. However, you are safe with me.

Jack *looks at him oddly with a "How did he hear me?" look.* **Vendor** *taps his ears.*

Vendor: Oh, how did I hear you? Natural ability—like sonar. You have nothing to fear. Crime is not something I believe in. Nor does anyone else. Except for criminals—they're a shifty bunch. *(Mary and Jack look at each other)* Speaking of which… *(Holds up some kind of small ceramic figurine)* could I interest you in an exquisite Scandinavian love goddess?

Jack: Well, I…

Mary: He means the doll.

Vendor: *(Covering the figure's ears or head)* Shhh! Not just a doll. She has the power to…

Mary: No, I don't think so. We've gotta…

Vendor: Okay, how about this necklace?

Mary: How pretty.

Vendor: This necklace comes from the Moo-Goo Too-Goo tribe in the heart of the Amazon rain forest. It promotes tranquility of both mind and spirit.

Jack: No, thank you, we don't want to…

Vendor: Okay, let's see…I know I've got something here that will interest you… *(At each of the following, Jack and Mary shake their heads)* Zen Garden? Bonsai tree? Rosary beads? Prayer shawl? *(Pause)* WWJD? bracelet? *(Pause)* I have a napkin that was prayed over by the…

Mary:	No. We don't want any of that stuff. Can we please go? We've got a train to catch.
Vendor:	No. You must tell me—do you believe in something? I've got something here from every faith, every religion.
Jack:	Well, let me ask you something: What do you recommend? Does any of it work for you?
Vendor:	No, no, no. Second rule of Street Vendor School: Do not become emotionally attached to the merchandise.
Jack:	Wait…second rule? What's the first?
Vendor:	Never try to sell things next to a Girl Scout cookie table.
Jack:	Oh…that makes sense. Who can resist a box of Do-Si-Dos™?
Mary:	Back to your second rule: "Don't get attached." So you're selling stuff that doesn't work?
Vendor:	Oh, sure, it all works. It just depends on you and how you view the supremeness of all things.
Jack:	But you don't believe in any of this stuff?
Vendor:	Oh, you could say I believe in all of it.
Jack:	Really?
Vendor:	Oh, yes.
Mary:	That seems like a lot to keep up with.
Vendor:	Yes, well, you see, there's some truth in all of it. As my mother taught me when I was very, very little, selling pencils at the bus station, "Always have your bases covered." That way, whatever happens after we die, you're taken care of.
Jack:	Huh?
Vendor:	Don't get left out on a technicality.
Mary:	I don't follow.

Vendor:	*(Getting frustrated)* Don't put all your eggs in one basket.
Jack:	Still not getting it.
Vendor:	*(Really frustrated)* Don't put your faith in a faltering fail-safe.
Mary:	Now you're just making things up.
Jack:	What's the point?
Vendor:	*(Put out)* There is no way you can know for *sure* if one way is the right way. So it's probably smart to believe in all of the religions just to make sure your eternal life is a good one!
Jack:	*(Finally understanding)* OH! So you mean we should always have our bases covered! You know, he's…uh…he brings up a good point.
Mary:	Yeah. Why gamble with eternity?
Vendor:	So are you interested in anything I've got to sell?
Jack & Mary:	*(Together, ad libbing)* Yeah, sure. Whatcha got? I'll take one of those, and one of those, and *two* of those… *(etc.)*

THE END

SKIT 1.4

"TRUE CRIME"

BY GINNYLEE ELLIS, WITH REVISIONS BY TOMMY WOODARD AND
EDDIE JAMES

WHAT: Luke goes to the police station to confess a crime. Although the police imagine that Luke's crime is something homicidal and drastic, it turns out to be a completely different sort of transgression.

WHO: Lt. Dawson, Sgt. Smith, Female Officer, Offender, Luke

WHEN: Present Day

WHY: Matthew 28:18-20; Romans 10:15

WEAR: (COSTUMES AND PROPS) Doughnuts, coffee mugs, cop gear, chairs, file folders

HOW: Play up this skit and give it all the creativity and energy you can. If you can get lighting effects, you'll want to turn them off quickly after the last line.

THEMES: Courage, Evangelism, Guilt, Confession

TIME: 5 to 7 minutes

The setting is a police station. **Sgt. Smith** *and* **Lt. Dawson** *enter.*

Dawson: Well, I tell you what Sgt. Smith, did you see it?

Smith: I sure did, Lt. Dawson! Fire, bullets—man, oh, man! It was the biggest chase scene ever. That there creator of *The Dukes of Hazzard* is a pure genius!

Female Officer: Got a shoplifter for you two.

Dawson: Okay, bring in the offender. I tell you what. This job doesn't get any easier, Sgt. Smith.

Smith: I totally agree with you, Lt. Dawson. What is this world coming to? You know, I was walking into my hair stylist's place, and this kid was trying to steal a 25-cent piece of candy from the machine.

Dawson: You've got to be kidding me! No way. You got your hair done? I knew something looked different.

Smith: Oh yeah, I go to Shelly. She's wonderful. She makes my scalp feel like no other stylist I've been to.

Female Officer: *(Clears throat, holds out file)* Excuse me Lieutenant, Sergeant, I have the shoplifter.

Dawson: Oh, thank you.

Smith: *(Opens the shoplifter's file)* Whew-ee. We have a repeat offender here, Lt. Dawson.

Dawson: I believe we do, Sgt. Smith. *(To **Offender**)* Do you know who we are?

Offender: *(Points with cuffed hands)* You are Lt. Dawson, and you are Sgt. Smith.

Dawson: What are you, a psychic?

Offender: No, you just called him Sgt. Smith.

Dawson: Don't get smart with me! We are the law. And we find those who break the law.

Smith: *(Interrupting)* Calm down and go in the corner for a second and find your happy place. Now what are we doing here today? You know that shoplifting is a no-no. *(Lt. Dawson clears throat)* Now just sit here and think about what you've done for a minute.

Dawson: Hey, what episode of *CSI Little Rock* was it where they pinpoint the tainted, poisoned doughnut? 'Cause I'm over there and want to know how to tell the difference between a poisoned and a non-poisoned pastry.

Smith: That's a toughie. Was it episode 16?

Dawson: Maybe. Or 37?

Smith: Nope, that was the one with the bear.

Offender:	Forget about it! *(Grabs the doughnut with cuffed hands and eats it)*
Dawson:	That's it! You are going into time-out mode right now! I don't want to hear a peep out of you!
Smith:	Man, oh, man, I tell you! What is goin' on around here?
Female Officer:	Hey, Bert and Ernie. I got a guy here that wants to confess.

Dawson *and* **Smith** *both react in surprise.*

Dawson:	Send him on in.

Luke *enters.*

Luke:	Um, hi.
Smith:	Why hello there, c'mon in. I'm Sgt. Smith and this is Lt. Dawson.
Luke:	I'm Luke.
Dawson:	Okay, that's Luke with an…
Luke:	L-U-K-E.
Smith:	Okay, and why are you here today? You weren't trying to steal a 25-cent piece of candy, were ya?

Dawson *and* **Smith** *laugh.*

Luke:	No, I…well…I can't do this. *(Tries to leave)*

Dawson *and* **Smith** *laugh.*

Dawson:	NO! *(They grab Luke and sit him back down)* Here, breathe. You can tell us anything.
Luke:	That's what I should have been doing! I should have told. I shouldn't have let it go this far.
Smith:	Whoa, calm down. We can work this out.
Dawson:	There's no reason to get your coif all crazy. If ya do, though, Sgt. Smith knows a gal named Shelly who will fix that hair of yours right up! Now, tell us what ya did.

Luke:	I didn't do anything.
Dawson:	I'm confused? What are you confessing?
Luke:	It's my roommate from college. His name is Ryan.
Smith:	Good, now we're getting somewhere.
Luke:	Well, we got along great and all. I couldn't have asked for a better roommate. We had a lot of fun pulling pranks against guys from the other dorms…
Dawson:	So where's the problem?
Luke:	He died. In a car accident.
Smith:	Were you driving?
Luke:	No.
Dawson:	Were you in the car?
Luke:	No.
Smith:	Then, son, I don't see any crime in the book to match.
Luke:	Don't you understand? He's dead…gone! And I don't know where he is. I went to church every Sunday. Every Wednesday. And I never once asked if he wanted to join me. Heck, I never even asked him what he believed in. I went to Bible studies, retreats, and other events, but I never asked him if he wanted to come. I never asked. Jesus said, "Go and make disciples." I don't even know if I know how to BE a disciple. I don't know about your book, but what I *didn't* do is a true crime in mine.
Smith:	Well, son, I'm sorry for your loss. But I can't do anything for you. The bottom line is that not sharing your faith is not a crime.
Luke:	It's not?
Smith:	Nope. It's not a crime.
Luke:	Well, it should be.

Lights down.

THE END

"WHAT IF?"
BY TOMMY WOODARD AND EDDIE JAMES

WHAT: Three people ask the question, "What if we stopped playing the 'What If' game and allowed God to use us instead?"

WHO: Male 1, Male 2, Female

WHEN: Present Day

WHY: Romans 8:15; 1 John 4:17-19

WEAR:
(COSTUMES AND PROPS) None

HOW: Keep the dialogue delivery real and not too dramatic. Have fun with the "fun" stuff. Make this skit your own.

THEMES: Fear, Courage, Trust, Faith

TIME: 3 to 5 minutes

Male 1: Everyone plays the "What If" game. What if I won a million dollars? Or what if I got the chance to go into outer space? Or what if I finally asked out that girl I've wanted to talk to all year? *(In character, to Male 2)* All right, here's all you have to say. *(Whispers in Male 2's ear)*

Male 2: You sure that will work?

Male 1: Positive, just go.

Male 2: *(To Female)* Hey, if I were a booger, would you pick me first?

Female: Get away from me, jerk. I don't want people to think I know you!

Male 1: *(To audience)* What if you could get her to say yes? *(To Male 2)* All right, so go up to her and say this: "Did it hurt?"

Male 2:	Did what hurt?
Male 1:	When you fell from heaven. Did it hurt?
Male 2:	Oh, that's gold.
Male 1:	I know. Or try this: "Are you tired?"
Male 2:	No, why?
Male 1:	Because you've been running through my mind all day!
Male 2:	Oh, that's good, too!
Male 1:	Okay, go talk to her.
Male 2:	*(Nervously, to **Female**)* Hey, I was just wondering, are you tired…or hurting…my mind…in heaven?
Female:	*(Says nothing, just turns away)*
Male 2:	*(To audience)* What if you quit listening to your friends for girl advice? *(To **Female**)* Hey, would you like to hang out sometime?
Female:	Yeah, sure!
Male 1:	*(To audience)* What if we didn't have anything special about us? What if we were just plain boring?
Male 2:	I can almost touch my tongue to my nose!
Female:	I can make some mean Kool-Aid!
Male 1:	My belly button is an outie!
Female:	*(To audience)* But what if we had great things about us; what if we had super powers?
Male 2:	Hey guys, check it out. I just figured out I have the power of being in two places at once!
Male 1:	No way!
Female:	Really?

Male 2:	Yeah, wait…you know that Italian restaurant down on 5th and Main?
Female:	Yeah?
Male 2:	Well, I'm eating the penne pasta, and it's wonderful! *(Burps)*
Male 1 & Female:	Wow, that's awesome!
Female:	Well, I just found out I have a super power, too! I can read people's minds!
Male 1:	No way!
Male 2:	Okay, well tell me what I'm thinking right now.
Female:	You're thinking that I can't actually read minds.
Male 2:	Wow, that's right!
Male 1:	That's what I was thinking, too!
Male 2:	*(To Male 1)* So dude, do you have a super power?
Male 1:	Yeah, umm…my belly button is an outie!
Male 2:	*(To audience)* Some super powers may be better than others.
Female:	*(To audience)* What if we questioned everything we knew?
Male 1:	What if none of this is real? What if this whole Christian thing were just some kind of hoax? What if there is no God?
Male 2:	What if there *is*? What if you're missing out on the greatest possible life?
Female:	What if I try to share the love of Jesus with people at my school? What if they think I'm a loser? What if I lose my friends?
Male 1:	What if no one else tells them? What if you let your fear be more important than your trust in God?
Male 2:	What if we quit playing the "What If" game? What if we pushed away all of our fears and let God take complete control of our lives? What if?

THE END

COMEDY

INTRO

Does This Smell Funny?

If something smells funny, does that mean it smells like a clown?

The truth is, some people read that question and laugh, and some people read that question and wonder what a clown smells like. That's because comedy is subjective. What some people find funny, others find dumb or objectionable. Therefore, it's *so* important that you know your audience and play to the funny bone with your comedy.

This new batch of comedy scripts has some great comedic moments. The authors who helped us with them are some of the funniest Christian writers we know. One of the keys for these scripts is to pay very close attention to whether you need to overdo it for bigger laughs or just let the dialogue do the work. You'll want the director to make that call because your actors will almost always want to overdo it!

As you read and use these scripts, keep a few things in mind: Comedy breaks down walls; it helps people lower their defenses; and it opens the doors to people's minds. Used effectively in Christian skits, comedy becomes a wonderful precursor to introducing the truth. And comedy, like any tool, can be used to build up…or tear down. We encourage you to use your comedic powers for good, not evil.

Skit Tips:

1. **Choose "the other white meat."** With comedy, you want to pick the "hams" from your group. As we stated in our previous book, *Instant Skits* (shameless plug!), improv or a comedic script is best handled by people who can make you laugh "offstage." These people are naturally the center of attention and don't mind taking risks, and they're the ones you want working your comedy. The truth is that people

who just don't know how to time a joke or wait for a laugh will not be successful at comedy—no matter how hard they try. So think of three to five "funny people" in your group—guys and girls—and ask them to join you. Face it: They'll make others laugh either from the stage or in the audience while you're trying to teach. So we suggest you harness their powers and use them for your good—or they may use it against you. (Why do you think our youth pastor finally asked us to be in skits?)

2. **Taste this and tell me if it's okay.** Aunt Nelda didn't cook using a recipe; she tasted whatever she was making and had other people taste it before she pronounced it "ready." Comedy works the same way. Before you put your actors onstage, *watch the skit*. Have others watch it, too. Did you laugh? Are the others laughing? If not, can you add or take away something from the mix? Even if the skit is hilarious, there may be some changes still worth making: Are there any ad-libs that need to become permanent parts of the skit? Are the actors out of control during a certain scene? With comedy, don't be afraid to "rein it in a bit." A skit can go from hilarious to offensive in 0.8 seconds. (And .01 seconds with a senior adult group!)

3. **Let the faint of heart stay home with Mama.** Comedy is a tough gig. We believe it's more difficult to pull off than drama, so take your comedy seriously! Comedy can also seem to take longer because actors want to milk the audience for every laugh they can get. In fact, good skits can go bad because actors thought they were the best part of the program and subsequently took over—and why not? Everyone was laughing! So, to avoid the Never-Ending Skit Syndrome, time the skit and be aware of its length. One of the most difficult things when producing comedy is deciding when to say when, but you can't go wrong by leaving an audience wanting more.

(And in case you're still wondering, a clown smells like cotton candy, happiness, and carny sweat!)

"BOMB SQUAD"

BY KNOX MCCOY

WHAT: A bomb squad specialist encounters an obstacle when an unexpected Guest appears during his latest emergency. Will he listen to the Guest's advice?

WHO: Sam, Bobby, Jesus

WHEN: Present Day

WEAR: A device resembling a classic movie bomb with red, blue, and green wires; a
(COSTUMES AND PROPS) pair of pliers; an apple

WHY: Psalm 22:4-5; Psalm 118:6-9

HOW: This skit examines how we can be indifferent or dismissive of God's presence in our lives when it seems as though things are "under control." Once trouble arrives, however, we quickly seek God.

THEMES: Trust, Reliance, Giving up Control, Wisdom, Listening

TIME: 7 to 8 minutes

The first sequence between **Sam** *and* **Bobby** *should be very tongue-in-cheek serious, almost melodramatic, soap-opera acting. Think Keanu Reeves on* Days of Our Lives.

Bobby: Okay, I think I've defused the trip line and the trigger switch has been disabled. We're getting close. How much time do we have left? *(Sam checks the front side of the device to gauge the time)*

Sam: Five more minutes. I'll call headquarters and get them to evacuate the block. You know… *(Throws a "soap opera serious" look over his shoulder)* just in case.

Bobby: *(Equally soap-opera serious)* Yeah, just in case. Listen, Sam. You're my friend and a good cop. But after you make that call, don't come back. You've done all you can, and the only thing left to do is a one-man job. I've got this.

Sam:	But…
Bobby:	No buts, Sam. I'm locking that door behind you.
Sam:	You're a stubborn man.
Bobby:	I'll see you on the flip side.

The two share an elaborate handshake. **Sam** *exits.*

Bobby:	*(Talking to himself)* Okay, here we go. Red wire, blue wire, green wire. What would MacGyver do? *(Breathes dramatically)*

Bobby *moves in cautiously with a pair of pliers and cuts the red wire.* **Jesus** *enters casually eating an apple, almost as if he stumbled upon this place.*

Jesus:	*(Bellows)* BOBBY! What's up?
Bobby:	*(Recoils in shock from the unexpected visitor and the tension of the situation)* HOLY Lord!
Jesus:	You got it. What's going on here?
Bobby:	Well, I…
Jesus:	I'm kidding. I already know. But you tell me—I want to hear your version.
Bobby:	*(Stares at **Jesus** for a couple of seconds and shakes his head)* Well, I'm kind of doing my job and trying to defuse this bomb. It was delivered to this house, and the wife heard a ticking noise, so they called me.
Jesus:	Interesting.
Bobby:	But I'm sure you'll be glad to know that I beat the first two traps— amateur work, if you ask me. And I was just about to disable the entire bomb when you startled me.
Jesus:	So you have this under control?
Bobby:	*(Laughs confidently)* Umm, yeah. I'd say I've got it under control.
Jesus:	Which wire are you cutting?

Bobby: *(Eye roll)* You know, I'm really kind of busy here. Do you…um…mind? *(Motions for **Jesus** to "shoo")*

Jesus: Oh yeah, yeah, no problem. I've got a crazy schedule today, so I'll just… *(Trails off)*

*Jesus moves to the edge of the stage while **Bobby** regains his composure and makes a dramatic show of preparing to cut the wire. Just as he's about to cut it, though…*

Jesus: Bobby!

Bobby: *(Very flustered—walks around shaking the nervousness out of his arms, hands, shoulders, etc.)* You CANNOT keep doing that! I'm trying to do my job here!

Jesus: I know, I know. I was just wondering if you'd ever seen that *MacGyver* episode when the bomb was booby-trapped with wires that were painted different colors, so he had to use a Tic-Tac and dental floss to disarm the bomb? *(Uses hand gestures to help **Bobby** understand there's a point to this story)*

Bobby: *(Thinks for a moment)* Oh yeah! I hated that episode. Too unrealistic. I mean, painted wires? Really? Were they kindergarten terrorists?

Jesus: *(Disappointed)* Riiiiiight.

Bobby: Seriously though, man.

Jesus: *Son of* Man.

Bobby: I really need you to leave. The clock is ticking here.

Jesus: Yeah, yeah, that's cool. No problem. I've got some prayers to answer, so I'll just catch up with you later… *(Trails off and retreats to the edge of the stage again)*

Bobby regains his composure once again and dramatically sets about cutting the wire. He finally cuts it and the lights on the device—or on stage—begin blinking ominously.

Bobby: Oh no! Good Lord in heaven, what am I going to do?!

Jesus: Listen, really, the name "Jesus" is fine. I'm actually not that big on the whole "title" thing.

Bobby:	*(Panicked)* What did I do? I thought the red wire disabled the entire thing!
Jesus:	Well, actually… *(Jesus pauses as though he has the correct answer)*… No, I'm sorry. This is your thing. I'm just butting in. I've overstepped.
Bobby:	What? No! TELL ME!
Jesus:	Bobby, are you asking for my help now?
Bobby:	YES!
Jesus:	You know, we could have saved some of these fireworks if you'd just asked for my help in the beginning.
Bobby:	I know, I know. But I thought I had it all under control.

Jesus and **Bobby** look at each other expectantly for a moment.

Bobby:	WELL?!
Jesus:	Oh, sorry. I thought you had more to say. Like maybe that you're thankful…
Bobby:	It can WAIT!
Jesus:	Well, here's the thing… *(Begins tinkering with the bomb)* you were right that the red wire was the one to cut. However, you didn't see that the "supposed" red wire was actually painted red to throw you off.
Bobby:	But how did you…
Jesus:	*(Stops working and looks around)* Really?
Bobby:	Right.
Jesus:	So when I cut the blue wire, which is actually the red wire painted blue… *(Cuts the wire; the lights stop blinking)* the bomb is disabled.
Bobby:	*(Leans back; wipes his brow)* Wow. That was close.
Jesus:	Listen, Bobby, you know I love you, right?
Bobby:	Yeah.

Jesus:	And you know I want to help you, right?
Bobby:	Yeah.
Jesus:	Well, why wait until things blow up—okay, sorry, bad choice of words— why wait until things are really bad before you seek my help?
Bobby:	I dunno. I guess I felt like I had everything under control.
Jesus:	Bobby, I want to help you! You just have to seek me out. This is what our relationship is for. We walk through life together, and I guide you through all the traps and trials that await you.
Bobby:	You're right. Thanks for helping me in spite of myself. *(Brief pause)* I can't believe I didn't pick up on your *MacGyver* reference.
Jesus:	Yeah, you totally whiffed there. What was that about?

As they exit the stage together...

Bobby:	Hey, speaking of help, we have this softball game next Thursday, and we could really use a good center fielder...

Lights down.

THE END

SKIT 22

"CALL ME 'SWEETNESS'"
BY BEN GAZAWAY

WHAT: This skit is a funny-but-pointed look at the mindset of those who spend most of their time thinking only about themselves.

WHO: Director, Justin Lemur (teen rock star), Makeup Girl, Hair Stylist, Intern (male or female), Cue Card Person (male or female)

WHEN: Present Day

WEAR:
(COSTUMES AND PROPS) Justin should be dressed like a pretentious rock star. You'll need a chair for the Director. The Hair Stylist and Makeup Girl need hair and makeup items to use on Justin. The Intern needs a clapboard. The Cue Card Person needs several posterboard cue cards and a black Sharpie®.

WHY: 1 Samuel 16:7; Proverbs 11:2; Philippians 2:3

HOW: This skit takes place in a make-believe television studio. The **Director** is sitting in a director's chair stage right. **Justin** is standing center stage, flanked by **Makeup Girl** and **Hair Stylist** who are busy primping him for the upcoming commercial shoot. Kneeling at the front center stage with his or her back to the audience is the **Cue Card Person** who simply holds the cue cards for **Justin** to read. Standing behind the **Director** is the **Intern** who's responsible for the clapboard.

THEMES: Humility, Wisdom, Selfishness, Selflessness, Fame, Materialism, Idols, Pride

TIME: 5 to 7 minutes

Lights up.

Director: Mr. Lemur, we appreciate your taking time out of your busy schedule to do this public service announcement…

Justin: Please…call me "Sweetness." *(Winks at the girls)* Everyone else does.

Director: Okay, Mr. Sweetness…

Justin: No, just "Sweetness"…it's just that I worked so hard to earn that name.

Director: *(Getting impatient)* Okay, "Sweetness," let's go over this. You're going to look into the camera, you're going to read what's on the cue card, and you're going to smile into the camera until I say cut. Do you have any questions?

Justin: Yeah, how much longer do you think this will take? *(Admiring the girls)* I'm having my Ferrari waxed as we speak.

Director: Well, that depends, *(With exaggeration)* "Sweetness," on how well you follow directions.

Justin: Let's get this over with. *(Again admiring the ladies)* Sweetness has more important things on his mind.

Makeup Girl *and* **Hair Stylist** *share a giggle.*

Makeup Girl: *(In a hushed, giddy voice)* Did you hear? He's having his Ferrari waxed!

Hair Stylist: *(In a hushed voice)* Ouch! That sounds painful.

They're interrupted by the **Director** *who sits down in his chair.*

Director: *(Yelling to everyone)* OKAY! QUIET ON THE SET!

The girls scurry away from **Justin**, *and the* **Intern** *steps in front of* **Justin** *with a clapboard.*

Intern: *(Yelling out)* Public Service Announcement, take one!

Intern *snaps the clapboard, and* **Justin** *looks at the audience.*

Justin: Hi, I'm Justin "Sweetness" Lemur. You might know me from my new Disney Channel hit show called *Hey, I'm a Teenager with a Rock Band*. We have a lot of fun on that show, but one thing Sweetness never jokes about…

Director: Cut! Justin, can you please not refer to yourself in the third person?

Justin: That's how Sweetness rolls, baby.

Director: Well, "Sweetness" is going to be here for a long time if "Sweetness" doesn't read what's on the cue card.

Justin: Fine, let's go...I'm feeling it this time.

Director *sits down;* **Intern** *comes back into the camera shot with the clapboard.*

Intern: *(Yelling)* Public Service Announcement, take two!

Intern *snaps the clapboard;* **Justin** *looks back out at the audience.*

Justin: Hi, I'm Justin "Sweetness" Lemur, star of the new Disney Channel show *Hey, I'm a Teenager with a Rock Band*. When I'm not rocking out for millions of beautiful girls, I'm thinking about my health. And there's nothing I take more seriously than carpet tunnel syndrome...

Director: CUT!

Makeup Girl *and* **Hair Stylist** *rush in to primp* **Justin's** *appearance.*

Director: Justin, it's not "carpet" tunnel syndrome; it's *carpal tunnel syndrome.* And can you please leave out that part about "millions of beautiful girls"? Just stick to the script.

Justin: *(Shooing the girls away)* Okay, I've got this, I've got this.

Director *sits down;* **Intern** *comes back into the camera shot with the clapboard.*

Intern: *(Growing tired and annoyed)* Public Service Announcement, take three.

Intern *snaps the clapboard again;* **Justin** *looks back out at the audience.*

Justin: Hey, I'm Justin "Sweetness" Lemur, star of Disney Channel's new hit show *Hey, I'm a Teenager with a Rock Band*. And when I'm not driving fast cars and hanging out with beautiful girls, I'm thinking about my health. And there's nothing I take more seriously than carpool tunnel syndrome...

Director: CUT! *(Exasperated)* Justin, it's "carpal"...

Justin: Carpool...

Director: Carpal...

Justin: Carport...

Director: Carpal...

Justin:	Carpe diem…
Director:	Okay, just repeat after me. Car…
Justin:	Car…
Director:	Pull…
Justin:	Pull…
Director:	Carpal…
Justin:	Farkle…

Director, *exasperated, snatches up the cue card and Sharpie® from* **Cue Card Person** *and starts writing.*

Director:	*(While he's writing)* Okay, "Sweetness," we're going to make this easy for you…just read the card.

Director *hands the cue card back to* **Cue Card Person** *and sits down. The* **Intern** *steps back in with the clapboard.*

Justin:	*(Getting himself psyched up)* Just read the card?
Director:	Just read the card.
Intern:	Public Service Announcement, take …whatever number we're on.

Intern *snaps the clapboard again;* **Justin** *looks back out at the audience.*

Justin:	Hi, I'm Justin "Sweetness" Lemur, star of Disney Channel's new hit show *Hey, I'm a Teenager with a Rock Band.* Today I want to talk about the importance of humility. You see, no matter how famous you are or how much money you have, recognizing that it all comes from God is the beginning of wisdom. Humility—it really is…sweetness… *(He ends on a cheesy smile)*
Director:	And cut! *(Standing to leave)* Very nice, Sweetness. I think we got what we needed.

Director *and* **Intern** *walk offstage;* **Makeup Girl** *and* **Hair Stylist** *rush in and take* **Justin** *by the arms as they stroll away.*

Hair Stylist:	That was amazing!
Makeup Girl:	I actually cried at the ending.
Justin:	It was pretty cool stuff, really.

They walk offstage, leaving only **Cue Card Person** *onstage. He or she then turns to the audience and holds up a posterboard cue card with the following Scripture written on it:*

Cue Card Person: "IF YOU REASON WITH AN ARROGANT CYNIC, YOU'LL GET SLAPPED IN THE FACE; CONFRONT BAD BEHAVIOR AND GET A KICK IN THE SHINS. SO DON'T WASTE YOUR TIME ON A SCOFFER; ALL YOU'LL GET FOR YOUR PAINS IS ABUSE. BUT IF YOU CORRECT THOSE WHO CARE ABOUT LIFE, THAT'S DIFFERENT—THEY'LL LOVE YOU FOR IT... SKILLED LIVING GETS ITS START IN THE FEAR-OF-GOD, INSIGHT INTO LIFE FROM KNOWING A HOLY GOD." (PROVERBS 9:7-12, MSG)

Lights down.

THE END

"COMMITMENT"
BY KNOX MCCOY

WHAT: This skit provides a look into human nature and the conditional ways we view our commitment to God and to others.

WHO: Alice, Frank, Minister

WHEN: Present Day

WEAR: The groom (Frank), Minister, and bride (Alice) should all be dressed in a manner loosely resembling a wedding ceremony. One ring is needed. A bouquet of flowers would be a nice touch.
(COSTUMES AND PROPS)

WHY: Although the skit is tongue-in-cheek, the larger point about the way we tend to be both cautious and flippant about our commitment to God is a very serious one.

HOW: Though the format is a wedding, this is an apt comparison to our relationship with God. We're okay with God as long as we aren't forced into uncomfortable positions. The setting should mirror a typical wedding ceremony, but the focus can be on the three characters.

KEEP IN MIND: As you prepare this skit, be aware that there are several voice-overs. You can accomplish this preparation in three ways:

Record your actors performing their voice-over lines beforehand and have your sound tech cue the lines at the appropriate time. This method requires a sound tech who pays very close attention to the skit.

Choose more actors to be backstage with microphones and do the voice-overs for those on stage. This approach will require you to find people whose voices closely match the voices of the actors performing the skit.

If neither of these first two choices is an option for you, then you can always have your stage actors do the voice-over lines live. However, if you do so, make sure the other actors freeze during these lines.

THEMES: Commitment, Sacrifice, Faithfulness, Marriage, Relationships, Loyalty, Covenant, Vows

TIME: 5 to 7 minutes

This skit should begin as a typical wedding ceremony. The first few lines from **Alice** *and* **Frank** *should be heard as a voice-over.*

Minister:	And that's when Alice here said, "So *that's* why the chicken crossed the road!" *(Raucous laughter)* And it was then that I knew these two kids are perfect for each other.
Alice:	*(Voice-over)* If I have to hear that story one more time, I'm going to peg him in the face with my bouquet. What is this, open mike?
Frank:	*(Voice-over)* What food did we decide on for the reception? I *really* want pigs in a blanket. Sausage balls would be nice too, though. I'm *so* hungry.
Minister:	It really is a wonderful day when two hearts can be joined together as one in front of such a large gathering of family and friends. The public declaration of love is essential to any marriage, and I urge you both to continue cultivating your love for everyone to see.
Alice:	*(Voice-over)* Why are you going off script?! This isn't an improv session! I will publicly cultivate a beat-down on you if you don't wrap it up!
Frank:	*(Voice-over)* You know who's underrated? Burt Reynolds. He was before his time. He'd be 10 times awesomer than Chuck Norris if only he'd come along a little later. What a tragedy.
Minister:	And now Alice and Frank, I've picked out a verse as you begin your lives together. In Ruth 1:16, Ruth says, "Entreat me not to leave you, *Or* to turn back from following after you; for wherever you go, I will go; and wherever you lodge, I will lodge; Your people *shall be* my people, And your God, my God." May that sentiment be the foundation for your marriage.

Frank:	*(Raises his hand)* Hey, quick question: What exactly do you mean by "the foundation for our marriage"? Would that be like saying the foundation of Burt Reynolds' career was his trademark grin and winning mustache?
Minister:	*(Taken aback by **Frank's** interruption)* Um…well…basically, like it says in the verse, it's important for each married couple to commit to each other beyond circumstance.
Frank:	Okay, but more specifically the part about her people being my people.
Alice:	Yeah, I was wondering about that, too.
Minister:	*(Hushed whisper)* Guys, is this really the time?
Frank:	Can you think of a better time? Get on with it!
Minister:	Well, basically it's about loyalty and commitment. You two have to immerse yourselves into every aspect of each other's lives.
Alice:	Whoa there! He's got some REALLY weird family members! They stuff all their pets after they die and set them around the house so it's like they're staring at you.
Minister:	I think you're missing the point.
Frank:	*(To **Alice**)* So we're going there? Well, at least my family doesn't think it's cool to show up at some random kitchen and start cooking other people's food. That's messed up.
Alice:	No, that's called volunteer work at a community kitchen, you idiot!
Frank:	Whatever, it's still weird!
Minister:	Guys! I think you're both a little stressed and sleep-deprived. Let's move on to the vows, and we can discuss some of these issues afterward.
Alice:	Good idea.
Minister:	Okay. Alice, will you place Frank's ring on his finger and repeat after me? *(**Alice** puts the ring on **Frank's** finger)*

Minister:	I, Alice, take you, Frank, to be my lawfully wedded husband…
Alice:	I, Alice, take you, Frank, to be my lawfully wedded husband…
Minister:	…to have and to hold, from this day forward, for better, for worse, for richer, for poorer…
Alice:	…to have and to hold, from this day forward, for better, for worse, for richer, for poorer…hey, let me stop you there. What exactly do you mean "for richer, for poorer"?
Minister:	Really?
Alice:	I mean, because what if one day he gets some disease that makes him go crazy, and then he comes home and starts lighting dollar bills on fire?
Minister:	I don't think that's a real disease, and anyway, the point is…
Frank:	How dare you compare me to Uncle Joe Bobby! That is *completely* unfair. The doctor said that illness skips a generation! So our kids could have it, but…I'm good.
Alice:	I just wanted some clarification on how literal these vows are. But please, go on.
Minister:	Okay, in sickness and in health, to love and to cherish, till death do us part. I pledge to you, my faithfulness.
Frank:	Hey, quick question about the whole faithfulness thing…
Minister:	*(Flabbergasted)* Of course.
Frank:	So let's say that Alice here becomes allergic to air, and she throws up if she breathes. Technically speaking, does God require me to stick with her? I mean, science has proven that air is everywhere, and I have a really sensitive gag reflex.
Alice:	How can someone be allergic to air, Frank?
Minister:	Guys…
Frank:	Well, I don't know, Alice, but I saw it on *The X-Files* once, so it must be true.

Alice:	The sound of your voice makes me crazy.

Frank and Alice ad-lib an argument about The X-Files, air allergies, Uncle Joe Bobby, etc.

Minister:	*(Finally can't take it anymore and yells out of frustration)* Enough! You two are incorrigible! *(Frank and Alice freeze—long pause as the three of them cut their eyes back and forth at each other)*
Frank & Alice:	*(Begin to defend themselves at the same time)* Well, we were just trying to…Don't misunderstand us…
Minister:	Shhh! Just stop. Enough. You two need to understand that marriage is a sacred vow made between you two and God. It's not about how you feel…feelings will go away. It's not about thinking you have everything figured out about each other…you'll soon find out that you *haven't* figured it all out. Marriage is about commitment. It's a commitment that if one of you gets sick—*any* kind of sick—you still stay together. It's a commitment that if you're wealthy beyond your dreams or poor beyond your nightmares, you still stick it out together. Until you figure that out, I cannot in good conscience finish this marriage ceremony. I'm sorry. *(Storms off)*

Frank and Alice are left standing onstage, awkwardly.

Alice:	So…we don't have to pay him, do we?
Frank:	We were going to pay him?
Alice:	Yeah.
Frank:	Didn't know that. So, do we still get to eat the pigs in a blanket and stuff?
Alice:	Somebody has to!
Frank:	*(Looks at audience)* Let's go eat!

Lights down.

THE END

"HEAR NO EVIL"

BY TED & NANCIE LOWE, WITH REVISIONS BY TOMMY WOODARD AND EDDIE JAMES

WHAT: Through the eyes of children, we see that others really are watching what we do and listening to what we say.

WHO: Becky, Timmy

WHEN: Present Day

WHY: Ephesians 4:29; Proverbs 4:23

WEAR: (COSTUMES AND PROPS) 2 Tricycles (optional)

HOW: The child characters in this skit can be played by actors of any age, but they should not be overplayed. For realistic characters, study children as they talk and play, and then model that behavior for this sketch. Childlike dialect is crucial here, but be very careful to articulate.

THEMES: Guarding Our Hearts, Mouths, and Minds; Relationships; Respect; Parenting

TIME: Approximately 3 to 5 minutes

Becky and **Timmy**, *both age 5, are playing "highway," making car noises and bumping into each other.*

Becky: Hey, get out of my way! *(Flings her arm up)*

Timmy: *(Imitates Becky's gesture, smiling)*

Becky: Timmy, you're not supposed to smile when you play Highway. *(Demonstrating)* You're supposed to honk your horn—BEEP! BEEP!— look at people real mean, and then fling up your arm.

Timmy: *(Attempting to demonstrate somewhat successfully)* Like this?

Becky:	That's a little bit better. *(They continue playing and making car noises until they bump into each other again.)* Hey, Jack! You got no business being on the highway! *(Flings her arm up again)*
Timmy:	I'm going home. *(Starts walking away)*
Becky:	*(Confused)* Why?
Timmy:	Because, Becky, you're being mean, and, and, and…that's MY job!
Becky:	No, I'm not. That's the way you're supposed to act on the highway.
Timmy:	Why?
Becky:	Well, that's what my big brother does when I ride in the car with him. *(Demonstrating)* He looks at people real mean, honks his horn—BEEP! BEEP!—and flings up his arm. But if my mommy's ever in the car, she tells him he'd better not be doing that—"especially in front of Becky." And then he says, "Why? It's my car!" And then she says, "No, it's not; it's *my* car." Then he tells her to shut up, and then she starts to cry, and then we all go to McDonald's®, and I play in the red balls at the play land.
Timmy:	*(Amazed)* Your brother tells your mommy to shut up?!
Becky:	Yeah, he tells her that all the time.
Timmy:	We're not allowed to say that at my house because one time my big sister told my mommy to shut up, and then my mommy said, "If you ever do that again, I'm knocking you into next week."
Becky:	What does that mean?
Timmy:	I don't know, but it sounds like it would hurt.
Becky:	Well, my big brother and my mommy are always screaming at each other. It scares me, and sometimes I start to cry; but Mommy says for me not to cry because it's not my fault.
Timmy:	*(Patting her shoulder as if to console her)* But it is your fault, Becky, because remember—you're the devil.

Becky: *(Very upset, getting louder as the line progresses)* Woooo, Timmy! You're not supposed to call me that! You got in trouble last time you called me that!! I don't know why I even play with you!!!

Timmy: *(Covering his ears, screaming)* Stop screaming! Stop screaming! *(Screaming)* My daddy says God does not want us to scream! *(Totally over it, smiling)* But my mommy can scream a lot louder than you can, especially at my big sister—she's in high school, and she's always getting in trouble. And my mommy screams at her and tells her to go to her room. And my sister runs into her room and slams her door and turns her music up real loud. And then her room goes *(Making motions with his hands as if the walls of the room are swelling in and out)* whoop, whoop, whoop, whoop! *(Very excited)* And one time, and one time, and one time she turned up her music so loud that it knocked a picture of my Nana off the wall and broked it!

Becky: *(Totally into his story)* Did that make your mommy cry?

Timmy: No, it made her scream even louder, and her face got red like this... *(Holds his breath to demonstrate, goes into the next line very excited)* And I said, "Mommy, Mommy, you look like the Red Power Ranger!" *(Immediately changes to sad disposition)* And then she put me in time-out.

Becky: Timmy, you tell the funniest stories.

Timmy: Well, I have to go home now.

Becky: *(Disappointed)* Why?

Timmy: I have to go sit in time-out.

Becky: Why, Timmy? What did you do this time?

Timmy: I got in trouble for drawing.

Becky: For drawing? What's wrong with that?

Timmy: Well, I got in trouble for where I was drawing and what I was drawing.

Becky: Oh...where were you drawing, and what were you drawing?

Timmy: I was drawing on the wall in the church, and I was drawing a picture of you.

Becky: Oh Timmy, you can't draw on the walls in the church! But it's sweet that you drew my picture.

Timmy: Yeah…the only problem is my drawing scared everybody.

Becky: Why did your picture of me scare everybody?

Timmy: 'Cause it looked like the devil 'cause that's what you are, Becky Nelson…you're the devil! (***Timmy*** *holds up devil horns behind his head and acts more funny/cartoony than scary as he chases **Becky** off-stage. All the while **Becky** is shouting, "Mommy!" and **Timmy** is saying, "I'm the devil!"*)

Lights down.

THE END

SKIT
25

"SUPERCHRISTIAN"
BY ROB COURTNEY

WHAT: An exaggerated look at how Christianity sometimes appears to the lost or hurting.

WHO: SuperChristian (male), BibleGirl (female), Homeless Person, Sad Lady, 3 Students

WHEN: Present Day

WEAR: SuperChristian and BibleGirl should be dressed in superhero costumes, including capes. All other characters should be dressed as their characters' identities suggest. One large book or Bible is needed, as well as a cell phone.
(COSTUMES AND PROPS)

WHY: Matthew 5:16; Luke 6:37; John 14:6; James 2:2-6

HOW: The SuperChristian and BibleGirl characters should be played with as much animation as possible, with many big gestures and huge egos in order to draw a contrast between them and the real-life characters.

THEMES: Truth, Witnessing, Beliefs, Love, Judgment

TIME: 5 to 7 minutes

Offstage voice or announcer: It's a saint! No, it's the Pope! No, it's Billy Graham! No, it's SUPER CHRISTIAN!

SuperChristian: Come, BibleGirl! We just got saved...that's right, I'm fresh out of the baptistery, and now I'm on a quest: To survive the world and make it to heaven! And you, young one, are fortunate to learn from me by becoming my sidekick!

BibleGirl: Holy acolyte! I'm so excited! On my way to heaven! I've got my Bible and...

SuperChristian: Well, you just worry about following me for now. I'm SuperChristian, and I know what I'm doing. Next stop: The golden streets of heaven!

They begin to walk; **Homeless Person** *enters.*

Homeless Person: Oh, I'm so lucky—SuperChristian is here! He will help me!

SuperChristian: He will?

BibleGirl: Holy opportunity, SuperChristian! Look! Someone needs our help, and we should...

SuperChristian: Leave! We should leave. We're on our way to heaven—remember, BibleGirl?

BibleGirl: But look! He's so cold...maybe we can at least give him your cape to keep him warm.

SuperChristian: What?! A superhero must look the part. I mean, if Superman took off his cape, do you know what he'd be?

BibleGirl: More practical?

SuperChristian: He'd be a flying speedo! I must have the cape so God knows what a Super Christian I am when I get to heaven.

BibleGirl: But in the book of James it says...

SuperChristian: *(Pushing **Homeless Person** away)* Good-bye now! Be warm and well-fed...just do it somewhere else. *(**Homeless Person** leaves)*

BibleGirl: That didn't feel too super, I really think...

SuperChristian: Shhhhh! Sidekicks don't think. They follow. So let's get going. We don't want to be late to heaven!

3 **Students** *enter and set about doing a religious ritual.*

BibleGirl: Holy misguided malpractice! Look, SuperChristian!

SuperChristian: No time for pictures, BibleGirl—we have to get to heaven!

BibleGirl: No, LOOK!

SuperChristian: What IS it, BibleGirl? Sweet Aunt Petunia's bridal bouquet! What is going on here?

Student: Oh hey, SuperChristian, we were just being religious. Oh yeah, and we believe Jesus isn't THE way—he's *A* way. So we're mixing up what we believe is true so we can have a more complete spirituality.

SuperChristian: Back, heathens! *(Hides behind **BibleGirl**)*

BibleGirl: I...um...I don't think that's the way it's supposed to be, SuperChristian. Don't you think we should talk to them about who Jesus really is?

SuperChristian: *(Still behind **BibleGirl**)* Yes, um...Jesus, not you! So...uh...stop?

BibleGirl: SuperChristian, we have to do more than that! *(To **Students**)* Look, kids, let me show you where the Bible says...

SuperChristian: BibleGirl, there's really no point. We should, you know, just let them do their thing while we do ours...mingling with outsiders could hurt us.

BibleGirl: But they look harmless...

SuperChristian: Oh sure, they start out that way just to lure you in. But we must view them as religious bug zappers: One minute they're nice and approachable, but the next minute—BAM! You have to scrape your theology off the wall!

Students: Well, it's time to go recruiting anyway. Who wants to be spiritual? *(They exit)*

BibleGirl: SuperChristian, we should have done something. They weren't dangerous—just in need of some guidance. And since we have the Truth, we have the authority to...

SuperChristian: Who retired and made you the captain? You just do your job and kick sides! I'll handle the rest.

Sad Lady *enters.*

BibleGirl: Holy weeping Wonder Woman!

SuperChristian: That's Wonder Woman?

BibleGirl:	Well, no. I just wonder why she's weeping.
SuperChristian:	Oh. *(Clears throat, then says boldly)* Stand back, BibleGirl! I'll handle this! *(To **Sad Lady**)* What's wrong, ma'am? Who did this to you? I'd be glad to show the villain the meaning of a good Old Testament stoning!
Sad Lady:	No one…well, everyone. I mean, I've had a hard life. I just got divorced, I don't know how I'm going to pay the bills this week, and my kids… they…I just need some help. At least someone to talk to and…
BibleGirl:	We're here to help, ma'am…
SuperChristian:	*(Astonished)* Well yes, BibleGirl, but there's no super villain to maim— except this woman, for her own mistakes. So maybe just a stern reprimand is in order… *(Points finger to scold **Sad Lady**)*
BibleGirl:	SuperChristian! She needs someone to support her through this hard time and show her love!
SuperChristian:	You're right, BibleGirl. I know just the guy. *(Pulls out a cell phone and has a brief conversation)* Okay, ma'am, I just called a preacher I know, and he'll take care of you. If you hurry up and get your act together, you can still make it to heaven with us! *(**Sad Lady** leaves in tears)*
BibleGirl:	Um, SuperChristian, I know I still have a lot to learn, but I thought we were supposed to, like, help others and…
SuperChristian:	That's enough, BibleGirl! You DO have a lot to learn…but we have to get to heaven. We found salvation, so now we just go on to heaven!
BibleGirl:	But SuperChristian…Jesus, the same guy who gave you salvation, said to do stuff like… *(Flips through Bible)*
SuperChristian:	BibleGirl! *(Snatches Bible away)* How do you expect to ever make it to heaven if we always stop to do everything in this book?! *(Throws down the Bible and leaves)*

Lights down.

THE END

DRAMA  3.0

INTRO

DRAMA: Less Is Really MORE

Have you ever left a movie and felt like you just witnessed some "great acting"? If you did, then it's likely that the actors' performances were so underdone that it *felt* like a huge bag of emotions even without the stereotypical "acting tricks." That's something to keep in mind as you work on these dramas. Even though you're onstage (most of you will be performing to audiences of 30 to 300), you can get away with not overdoing it. We're not saying you should be drab onstage, but figure out how to find small nuances that make your character more "real." If you feel like you're "acting," you probably are. Just try talking through the lines as a normal conversation and go from there.

For this new batch of dramas, we picked some doozies. Some will make you cry, some will make you ache, some may even make you uncomfortable—but all of them will make you think. With these skits you'll want to use your best actors—your "go-to" people or the ones you know can play it *up* without *over*playing it. (Yes, we're repeating ourselves.)

Keep in mind that some of these skits don't "ride off into the sunset"; rather they're designed to feel more like real life where people don't always choose the right thing in the end. Also, as in real life, these skits may contain some humor. Like the drama, the humor should be played more naturally, not over-the-top.

Be careful with your dramatic skits. They'll either be the best things you do or the worst; with drama, there's often no middle ground.

Behold! The Drama Boundaries

1. **Don't act like a recently grounded 13-year-old.** Actors in a dramatic role often end up overacting by exaggerating their expressions and movements. They yell when

a whisper would be more powerful. They say and do things no sane person would say or do in real life. We're not pointing fingers here; it's natural to want to make a dramatic role a heavier performance. The key is to remember the golden rule in drama: *Less is more.* (See? We said it again.) Let the script provide the drama—to overdo it is to kill it.

2. **Not "WWJD?" but "WWTCD?"** In life, it's always a good idea to put ourselves aside and try to behave as Jesus would. But on the stage, we need to choose to inhabit *the characters we're playing*, put our own opinions and reactions away, and even give Jesus a rest. (Unless you're playing the role of Jesus—in which case, WWJD? your little heart out!) The question isn't how would *you* react to a situation or say the dialogue, but how would *that character* react or say it? This is a difficult distinction to make, but one that's critical to drama. We tend to put ourselves in the *situation* instead of putting ourselves in the *character*. If someone walks away from your performance and believes *you* just got mad and yelled onstage, then you've missed the mark. But if audience members can lose themselves in the person you're playing, then you've accomplished your goal.

3. **Hurry up and slow down!** We know that doesn't make sense, but it got your attention, right? The point is to slow down. Too often actors tend to rush through the skit, zipping dialogue back and forth until the scene sounds more like Ping-Pong™ with words. Try to play the scene at the appropriate rhythm and tempo of a real-life scenario. In most cases, that means to go slower than you think you should. By the way, while you're slowing down, don't be afraid to shut your trap and let your face do some acting. Don't tell us what happened; *show* us with your eyes and facial expressions. On the old television show *Friends*, Joey used to call it "smell the fart" acting, but we don't use that kind of language.

4. **Robert De Niro and Meryl Streep you are not.** What is it about stepping on stage that turns a lot of actors into Shakespearean rejects with British accents? A major *faux pas* of dramatic acting is the distortion of dialogue due to over-enunciation. With dramas, the more naturally you speak, the better it will come across. Let's face it: Most of us haven't studied at Juilliard, and we aren't flipping through this book between Broadway casting calls. So just be natural. Think about how your character would speak and try not to chew up your dialogue until it's unrecognizable. The more relaxed you are, the more realistic your character will be.

"I LOVE YOU NO MATTER WHAT"

BY TED & NANCIE LOWE, WITH REVISIONS BY TOMMY WOODARD AND EDDIE JAMES

SKIT 3.1

WHAT: A young girl strays away from God...can she ever come back?

WHO: Teardrop 1, Teardrop 2, Ben, Beth

WHEN: Present Day

WEAR: (COSTUMES AND PROPS) 2 stools, 2 chairs, 2 backpacks, miscellaneous items for the backpack (Bible, pens, gum, etc.), as well as an iPod or iPhone

WHY: Matthew 5:13; Luke 15:11-28

HOW: This sketch is more complicated than most. To keep the sketch moving, the **Teardrops** must communicate with feeling and a natural sense of ease. Your team will also need to pick a slow song for the last scene. The last scene is critical and should be played slowly and with appropriate expression. Have several people watch the sketch before its presentation to help with the clarity and understanding of the piece.

THEMES: Faithfulness, Acceptance, Friendship

TIME: 10 minutes

Scene One: *Sarah McLachlan's "Angel" plays in the background for 15 seconds, then fades down. The scene opens with* **Teardrop 1** *and* **Teardrop 2** *sitting on stools.*

Teardrop 1: What an intense life I led. All my life consisted of was waiting for my big moment—never really knowing what that moment would be. Would it be a moment of joy, a moment of happiness, a moment of sadness? Whatever it was, my job was to wait. My life was to wait. Because, you see, I am a teardrop, and that is what teardrops do. They wait to be shed. Unfortunately, my big moment—the moment I'd always waited for, the moment I was shed—was a moment of regret. I was shed by a girl named Beth.

You see, for a long time I really thought I'd be shed for something joyous; something incredible! Why? Because Beth was joyous and incredible. I remember when Beth was about 13. She was sitting on a bus, about to leave for church camp, when a boy her age walked onto the bus…and, well…why don't you just see for yourself…?

Scene Two: Beth *is sitting on one chair with an empty chair beside her, as if she's sitting on a bench seat of a bus.*

Beth:	*(Going through her backpack, merrily singing with her headphones on, pops some gum into her mouth)*
Ben:	*(Enters looking somewhat nervous, wearing his backpack)* Is anyone sitting here?
Beth:	I'm sorry, I can't hear you.
Ben:	*(A little louder)* I said, "Is anyone sitting here?"
Beth:	*(Removing one of her headphones)* What's that?
Ben:	*(Almost screaming)* I said, "Is anyone sitting here?!"
Beth:	*(Removing both headphones)* I'm sorry, I still can't hear you. But you're going to want to take a seat. The bus is about to leave.
Ben:	Why didn't I think of that? *(Sits down)*
Beth:	*(Removes headphones completely)* Hi, I'm Beth McKinsey. What's your name?
Ben:	Ben Sparks.
Beth:	That's a funny name.
Ben:	What's so funny about it?
Beth:	Ben Sparks? Does anyone ever call you "Sparky"?
Ben:	No!
Beth:	Well, they should. Sparky is a great name.
Ben:	Sure, a great name…for a dog.

Beth:	It sounds like your new nickname. That's it—your new nickname is Sparky. I will announce it to the bus, and by the time we get to camp, everyone will be calling you Sparky. *(Stands to announce it)* Hey, everybody! This is my new friend…
Ben:	*(Grabs **Beth's** arm and pulls her back down, then puts his hand over her mouth, holds it a while, and lets go)*
Beth:	Spar…
Ben:	*(Covers her mouth again, then lets go)*
Beth:	Spar…
Ben:	*(Covers it again)* If I let you go, will you promise not to say it?
Beth:	*(Nods her head in the affirmative)*
Ben:	Do you promise?
Beth:	*(Rolls her eyes, but crosses her heart with her finger)*
Ben:	*(Releases her mouth)*
Beth:	Sheeewww… *(Stands, speaking fast)* Hey, everybody! This is my new friend Sparky…everybody say, "Hi, Sparky!"
Ben:	*(Very embarrassed)* You are crazy.
Beth:	No, I'm not. I just gave you a great nickname…Sparky. Everybody needs a nickname. Your name is going to sound great in the song.
Ben:	I'm going to hate myself for asking this, but what song?
Beth:	You know, the song that goes: "Sparky Sparky Bo Barky, Banana Fanna Fo Farky, Me My Mo Marky…Sparky!"
Ben:	You are crazy.
Beth:	I've never seen you at youth group before…where did you come from?
Ben:	I think that's a question I should be asking you…
Beth:	Ha ha, very funny. Where did you come from?

Ben:	My dad got transferred here.
Beth:	Do you like it?
Ben:	It's okay. I just don't know anyone.
Beth:	You know me.
Ben:	Like I said, I just don't know anyone.
Beth:	That was mean…but very funny.
Ben:	I'm sorry. I just haven't made a lot of friends yet.
Beth:	Well, I'd be honored to be the very first. *(Sticks out her hand)* Beth McKinsey.
Ben:	*(Reluctantly shakes her hand)* Ben…
Beth:	*(Interrupts him)* Sparky!
Ben:	*(Smiling)* Whatever.

Scene Three: *Focus returns to* **Teardrop 1** *and* **Teardrop 2** *sitting on their stools.*

Teardrop 1:	From that day on, Beth and Ben—or should I say "Sparky," since that's what everyone else called him—were the best of friends.
Teardrop 2:	As you've already heard from my friend here, it's tough to be a teardrop…never knowing what you'll be shed for. I wanted to be shed for something great; something important. So I waited and waited, praying I wouldn't be shed in vain…shed for something silly. I got my wish—I was shed for something important. But it was something sad. I rolled down the cheek of a guy named Ben. I was shed when his friend Beth did something really hurtful.
	But before that, I was sure I'd be shed for something great…because Ben was great. Ben loved Jesus. He stayed faithful to God for his entire high school career. Ben loved God, and he loved being alive, so I just knew that I'd be shed for something amazing. But again, I wasn't; it was just something important. But before "it" happened, Ben and Beth were the best of friends.

Scene Four: Beth and Ben *are on the phone with each other.* **Ben** *is pacing;* **Beth** *is relaxed but getting ready to go out.*

Ben: Should I ask her, Beth?

Beth: Yes, yes, for the 99th time—you should ask Lisa to go out with you.

Ben: What if she says no?

Beth: Believe it or not, Ben, the world will stay on its axis and continue to turn.

Ben: But if she says no, I'll feel like the world's biggest jerk.

Beth: Ben, you *are* the world's biggest jerk.

Ben: *(Not really listening)* I know. *(Realizing what **Beth** said)* What? *(Pause)* That was funny. But what if she says no?

Beth: *(Stalling)* Then…

Ben: Then what…?

Beth: If not, then…

Ben: Then what?

Beth: Then we'll put a bag over your head and pray for the best…

Ben: Very funny.

Beth: Ben, would you relax? This is not that big of a deal. Look, you believe God has a plan and everything happens for a reason, right?

Ben: *(Still pacing, chewing his nails)* Right…

Beth: Then if it's meant to be, she'll say yes.

Ben: Yeah, I guess you're right.

Beth: I'm always right.

Ben: You're right. You're completely right.

Beth: The sooner you learn that, the better.

Ben:	Well, I'm going to do it—I'm going to call her.
Beth:	Call her.
Ben:	Hey, Beth…
Beth:	Yeah?
Ben:	Thanks for being my friend.

Scene Five: *Focus returns to* **Teardrop 1** *and* **Teardrop 2** *sitting on their stools.*

Teardrop 2:	They were great friends. The type of friendship you just know God smiled upon. They loved God, and they loved to laugh. But then something happened. To most, it seemed out of the ordinary…
Teardrop 1:	…but to me, Beth's teardrop, I began to see it coming. When Beth was little and even early on in high school, she was incredibly joyous. But something began happening to her. Again, she loved Jesus, and she was walking with him. But some people didn't like that about Beth, and they started to let her know it. They'd say, "Come on, Beth, you're so much fun—don't hang around with those goody-goodies. Come with us." At first she said no. But then she started liking the fact that the "Who's Who" of the school paid attention to her. They made her feel special and important. She liked feeling popular. So she started—just a little bit, mind you—to hang out with them. Then one day she took her newfound popularity just a little bit too far…

Scene Six: **Ben** *and* **Beth** *pass each other in the hallway, and she ignores him.*

Ben:	Hey, Beth! Are you…
Beth:	*(She ignores him)*
Ben:	Beth, are you…
Beth:	*(Still ignoring him)*
Ben:	Beth!
Beth:	Oh, I'm sorry, Ben. I didn't see you… Listen, I've really got to go…
Ben:	Yes, you did.

Beth:	Yes I did what?
Ben:	You saw me.
Beth:	No, I didn't. Don't be ridiculous.
Ben:	Yes, you did. You saw me, and that's about the fourth time you've ignored me in the past two months.
Beth:	You're being paranoid.
Ben:	No, I'm not. You ignore me in the lunchroom when you're with your new friends, you never return my phone calls, you...
Beth:	Oh, I'm sorry. You're right, Ben, you're not paranoid. You're *jealous*.
Ben:	*(Exasperated)* What?
Beth:	You're jealous. You're jealous that I've made some new friends.
Ben:	No, I'm not.
Beth:	Yes, you are. All we talk about in youth group is reaching out to our lost friends. Well, how are we going to reach them if we don't have any?
Ben:	I don't think you're reaching them, Beth. I think they're reaching you.
Beth:	What's that supposed to mean?
Ben:	*(More calmly)* You're different, Beth. You're kind of...
Beth:	What?
Ben:	Nothing.
Beth:	No—if you have something to say, say it!
Ben:	*(Angry again)* You're like their puppet.
Beth:	What?
Ben:	You are. You change with the wind, to be whatever they want you to be.
Beth:	I do not.

Ben:	You do too. *(Pause)* It's just that I miss you, Beth.
Beth:	Well, I don't miss you, and I don't miss all those losers at church trying to tell me what I should and shouldn't be doing, okay?
Ben:	*(Walks away)* Fine!
Beth:	Ben, come back. I didn't mean it! Come back…Sparky…

Scene Seven: *Focus returns to* **Teardrop 1** *and* **Teardrop 2** *sitting on their stools.*

Teardrop 2:	Yes, I was shed by Ben that day. Beth was his best friend, and she'd traded him in for some new models. He was crushed, and I was shed. That wasn't exactly the way I wanted to be shed, but that was the way it happened.
Teardrop 1:	That was the way it happened all right, and Beth felt terrible. That afternoon she shed me and about a million more just like me. She knew her new friends had pulled her away from her old friends; but more importantly, they'd pulled her away from God. They pulled her away from being the person God had created her to be—Beth, a joyous, incredible girl who loved Jesus and everybody else. She wondered if she could she ever go back to the way it used to be. Could she ever go back to being that person again?

Scene Eight: *The last scene is acted without words. It begins with a song playing in the background. (Choose a song that would work well, whether secular or Christian.)* **Ben** *walks out while looking for something in his backpack.* **Beth** *enters from the opposite side.* **Ben** *sees her out of the corner of his eye. He ignores her, but she slowly walks over to him. They have a bit of a discussion. You can see subtle anger and disappointment on* **Ben's** *face.* **Beth** *is meek and trying to explain herself. He finally motions for her to come over, and she lays her head on his chest. He puts his arms around her in a friendship-style fashion. Then* **Ben** *grabs* **Beth's** *hand and they exit the stage together.*

THE END

"I'M NOT BEAUTIFUL"

SKIT
32

BY REBECCA WIMMER, WITH REVISIONS BY TOMMY WOODARD AND EDDIE JAMES

WHAT: Three young girls allow windows into their thoughts and why they don't like what they see in the mirror.

WHO: Girl 1, Girl 2, Girl 3

WHEN: Present Day

WEAR: 1 belt for each girl
(COSTUMES AND PROPS)

WHY: Psalm 45:11; Psalm 139:13-18; Ephesians 1:4

HOW: The three actresses should stand side by side onstage and speak directly to the audience. Utilize the belt as a symbolic costume piece. Whenever all three speak in unison, each girl should tighten her belt repeatedly until the very end, at which point the belts will become thoroughly uncomfortable.

THEMES: Self-Esteem, Identity, Comparison, Body Image, Eating Disorders

TIME: 6 minutes

Girl 1:   I'm not beautiful. I'm not.

Girl 2:   My mom says I am. But that's my mom.

Girl 3:   She's supposed to say that.

Girl 1:   They say God thinks I'm beautiful.

Girl 3:   But God's supposed to say that too.

Girl 1:   I'm not beautiful.

Girl 2:   And it's more than not having the right jeans…

Girl 3:	The right haircut…
Girl 1:	The right this or that.
Girl 3:	I just don't feel beautiful.
Girl 2:	And I don't know how to feel beautiful.
Girl 1:	Is it a new shirt?
Girl 3:	Or a cute pair of shoes?
Girl 2:	A new haircut?
Girl 3:	That helps for a while.
Girl 1:	But then I look in the bathroom mirror.
Girl 3:	I catch a glimpse of myself in a window.
Girl 2:	I see another girl…
Girl 3:	And I don't look skinny.
Girl 1:	I don't look cute.
Girl 2:	I look fat.
Girl 1:	I feel fat.
Girl 3:	I'm so fat.
Girl 2:	Fatter than yesterday, I think.
Girl 3:	Maybe it's the pockets on these pants.
Girl 2:	Maybe it's this color I'm wearing.
Girl 1:	Maybe it's…no…it's me.
Girl 3:	And I think maybe I'd be prettier if I were just five pounds lighter.
Girl 2:	Five pounds.
Girl 1:	How many missed meals would that be?

Girl 3:	Three?
Girl 1:	Five?
Girl 2:	Ten?
All:	I could do that. *(Tighten belts)*
Girl 2:	It's just a few missed meals. There's nothing wrong with that, right?
Girl 3:	No harm in that.
Girl 2:	And I'd be five pounds smaller.
Girl 3:	Five pounds prettier.
Girl 1:	Five pounds closer to perfect.
Girl 3:	That would fix everything.
Girl 1:	Then, I'll be beautiful.
Girl 2:	But then I spot myself in that mirror again.
Girl 3:	I see myself in that windowpane.
Girl 1:	I see another woman I think is beautiful.
Girl 3:	Ten pounds.
Girl 1:	Ten pounds, and I'll stop feeling this way.
Girl 2:	Then I won't think I'm so ugly.
Girl 1:	*So* not beautiful.
Girl 3:	So fat.
Girl 1:	Then boys will like me.
Girl 3:	Then people will like me.
Girl 2:	I'll fit into smaller jeans.
Girl 3:	I'll fit into a smaller skirt.

Girl 1:	I'll fit in.
Girl 2:	It's just 10 pounds.
Girl 3:	How many lunches is that?
Girl 2:	How many dinners?
Girl 1:	Breakfasts?
Girl 2:	Ten?
Girl 3:	Maybe 12?
Girl 1:	Maybe 20?
All:	I could do that. *(Tighten belts)*
Girl 2:	It's just for a little while.
Girl 1:	Because picture day is just around the corner.
Girl 2:	The dance is just around the corner.
Girl 3:	Our beach trip is just around the corner.
Girl 2:	Ten pounds.
Girl 1:	Ten pounds smaller.
Girl 2:	Ten pounds prettier.
Girl 3:	Ten pounds closer to perfect.
Girl 1:	But…it's right around the corner.
Girl 3:	Maybe I need to miss 20 meals.
Girl 2:	Or 30 meals.
Girl 1:	Or 40.
Girl 3:	But my mom will know.
Girl 1:	My dad will figure it out.

Girl 2:	My friends will think something's up.
Girl 1:	I bet my friends won't say a thing.
Girl 3:	Fifteen pounds, then.
Girl 2:	I'll drink juice.
Girl 1:	I'll drink coffee.
Girl 3:	I hear smoking keeps your weight down.
All:	I could do that. *(Tighten belts)*
Girl 1:	Because I want to be beautiful.
Girl 3:	Like the pictures in the pages and on the screen.
Girl 2:	I know they're airbrushed.
Girl 3:	I know they're doctored.
Girl 1:	In my head I know they're not really real, but…
Girl 2:	I want to be beautiful.
Girl 3:	Because I see how the boys look at her.
Girl 3:	She's so beautiful.
Girl 1:	I know all the guys wish they were with her, and she's so much prettier than I am.
Girl 2:	I want to feel beautiful.
Girl 3:	I want to stop feeling this way.
Girl 1:	How many pounds did I say?
Girl 2:	Twenty?
Girl 1:	Yeah, 20.
Girl 3:	Twenty pounds smaller.

Girl 1:	Twenty pounds prettier.
Girl 2:	Twenty pounds closer to perfect.
Girl 3:	Then I'll feel beautiful.
Girl 1:	Then I'll BE beautiful.
Girl 2:	And if not…
Girl 3:	Make it 25.
All:	I could do that. *(Tighten belts for the last time. Beat)*
Girl 1:	Someone please…
All:	Tell me I'm beautiful.
Girl 3:	Someone, please…make me believe it.
Girl 2:	God, I want to be beautiful.
Girl 1:	*(Looking up to heaven)* Why didn't you make me beautiful?

THE END

"RING AROUND THE ROSIE"

BY TOMMY WOODARD AND EDDIE JAMES

WHAT: Over the course of a school year, two friends become distant acquaintances as spiritual apathy slowly takes over one of them.

WHO: Jack, Bill

WHEN: Present Day

WHY: Deuteronomy 5:19; 2 Chronicles 7:14; Romans 12:2

WEAR: 1 chair
(COSTUMES AND PROPS)

HOW: This skit is very powerful if the actors find the gravity of the characters' emotions and concerns. If it's played melodramatically or over the top, the audience will disconnect themselves from the skit.

THEMES: Friends, Repentance, Accountability, Giving Up, Excuses

TIME: 6 to 8 minutes

Jack and **Bill** address the audience.

Jack: Jack and Bill went up the hill to get closer to their Lord…

Bill: Jack stayed strong fairly long, but Bill…he quickly got bored.

Both: *(Singing to audience)* Ring around the rosie,
A pocket full of posies,
Ashes, ashes,
We all fall down.

Jack: *(To audience, state the current date plainly and simply. The date will keep changing as the spiritual apathy sets in.) (To **Bill**)* Whoo! *(Name of occasion/camp)* This has been an amazing time!

Bill:	Wow! What a great _____ *(Name of event)*! We are different people now, right!?
Jack:	Yes! I'm so glad God spoke to us. Life is going to be different now...
Bill:	I feel like God's really changed me!
Jack:	Now, I want you to keep me accountable. Ask me how I'm doing on the tough stuff in my life. No holding back.
Bill:	I will, and you do the same for me, too! Come on in for a hug. Love you, buddy.
Jack:	*(Overcome with emotion)* Love you, too. *(Make this comical)* Give me another hug!

They hug, clearly on an emotional high.

Both:	*(Singing, to audience)* Ring around the rosie, A pocket full of posies, Ashes, ashes, We all fall down.
Jack:	*(State the date to the audience—needs to be **two months later**) (To **Bill**)* Bill, how're you doing?
Bill:	Good, man. How're you?
Jack:	Good...how're classes?
Bill:	They're going pretty good. Struggling a bit in Algebra, but that figures.
Jack:	Yeah. How're your times with God going?
Bill:	Pretty good. I mean, I was studying in Ephesians today...it was just awesome.
Jack:	Yeah. *(Notices someone)* Isn't that Jennifer?
Bill:	*(Sees her, too)* Yeah, it is. *(Calls out)* Hey, Jennifer!
Jack:	Hey, Jen! *(They both look shocked)*
Bill:	Hey, that was a look, wasn't it?

Jack: That was total "stink eye"! Didn't she go to _____ *(Name of event)* with us?

Bill: Yeah, but I heard once we got back from *(Name of event)*, she went to a party (**Note to Director:** *If the word "party" is too trite or cliche, change it to something else*), and it's been downhill ever since.

Jack: Is that right?

Bill: Yeah.

Jack: Did you get invited to that other party *(Change the word "party" if something else fits better)* this Friday night?

Bill: Yeah. Did they invite you?

Jack: Yeah. I told them I'm not gonna go. It will be hard, but I have to start making wiser choices.

Bill: Yeah.

Jack: *(Off **Bill's** look)* Did you *not* say no?

Bill: Well…I kind of said no. I did. I said, I didn't *know*, you know, but…

Jack: You're not gonna go, are you?

Bill: I don't know. I'm thinking I might go. I thought it might be a good way to reach out to Jennifer and get her involved again.

Jack: Is there anything I can do for you? 'Cause I know the stuff that makes you fall back into the "old ways…"

Bill: Don't you worry. I'll have a bottled water in my hand, and I'm strong. Just pray for me, okay?

Jack: Okay. I love you.

Bill: I love you too, man.

Both: *(Singing. This time **Jack** sings normal, but **Bill** sings slower, with less energy, and sits in a chair)* Ring around the rosie,
A pocket full of posies,
Ashes, ashes,
We all fall down.

Jack:	*(To audience)* December 14, 20—. *(To **Bill**)* Bill!
Bill:	*(A tad lethargically)* Hey, man. What's going on?
Jack:	I haven't seen you since, I think, Thanksgiving. How've you been?
Bill:	I've been okay. I've been doing okay.
Jack:	Merry Christmas!
Bill:	Thanks. Oh! I heard you were going to be in that Christmas program at your church.
Jack:	It's your church, too.
Bill:	Yeah, I meant our church.
Jack:	Are you gonna come?
Bill:	I may have to work, but I'll try, okay?
Jack:	I gotta ask you a question…um, we were accountability partners, y'know, since *(Name of event)*, and I've just heard that you've been slipping back into some stuff. And well, you told me that if I ever heard anything to come to you, so…is everything okay?
Bill:	*(Slowly)* Yeah. I mean yeah, I've been missing time with the Lord, but I'm not into drugs or anything. Don't worry. I'm just taking a break.
Jack:	Okay. Is there anything I can do for you?
Bill:	Yeah…why don't you pray for me, okay?
Jack:	Okay. I love you.
Bill:	Yeah, me too.
Both:	*(Singing—again, **Jack** is strong, but **Bill** has become even slower and ends up seated on the floor)* Ring around the rosie, A pocket full of posies, Ashes, ashes, We all fall down.

Jack:	*(To audience)* March 14, 20—. *(To **Bill**. Concerned)* Bill! I thought that was you. How're you doing?
Bill:	*(With a weak smile)* I'm a little…I'm here.
Jack:	We were just talking about you the other day, wondering how things were. We miss you at church.
Bill:	Yeah. Yeah. I miss you all, too. *(Defensive)* Y'know, you don't have to go to church to be a Christian, okay? I mean I think you probably learned that at *(Name of event)*.
Jack:	I kn…
Bill:	*(Interrupting)* Besides, there are a lot a hypocrites there. People look down on me 'cause I haven't been to church in a while…
Jack:	I was…I just wanted to tell you that God loves you and that you're never too far away that he can't grab you.
Bill:	*(Unaffected)* Yeah, that's cool.
Jack:	Bill, is there anything I can do for you?
Bill:	Ah, no, man, no.
Jack:	I love you.
Bill:	Yeah.
Both:	*(Singing. This time **Bill** is slumped on floor)* Ring around the rosie, A pocket full of posies, Ashes, ashes, We all fall down.
Jack:	*(To audience)* May 14, 20—. *(To **Bill**)* Hey, Bill. Some people said you were here. *(Pause. Deep concern)* How you doing?
Bill:	*(Very passive)* I'm okay.
Jack:	You know, as your friend, you don't look okay.
Bill:	Look, man, don't worry about me.

Jack:	I can't help it. I keep thinking how much Jesus would go after you. I'm not giving up on you.
Bill:	Don't worry about me, okay?
Jack:	Don't you remember the commitment you made?
Bill:	Yeah, I know. Are you through preaching?
Jack:	I'm sorry. I wasn't meaning to. God loves you, Bill. *(Silence)* Is there anything I can do for you? *(Silence)* I love you.
Both:	*(Singing, **Bill** slowly stands)* Ring around the rosie, A pocket full of posies… *(Spoken)* Ashes, ashes, Will you fall down?
Jack:	Jack and Bill went up the hill to get closer to their Lord.
Bill:	To be like Jack, you should strive to keep your faith alive.
Jack:	Because to be like Bill…you just can't afford.

THE END

"SMALL TALK"

BY CARRIE VARNELL, WITH REVISIONS BY TOMMY WOODARD AND EDDIE JAMES

SKIT

34

WHAT: This skit illustrates how easy it is to really miss what's going on in the life of a friend.

WHO: Lucy, Amy

WHEN: Present Day

WEAR: 2 backpacks, facial tissue
(COSTUMES AND PROPS)

WHY: Proverbs 17:17; 18:24; Matthew 5:14

HOW: This skit has a catch to it: Lucy needs to perform her lines *exactly* the same way in both scenes. And Amy's lines in Scene Two represent what people *really want* to say when someone asks, "How are you?"

THEMES: Listening, Friendship, Trials, Stress, Suicidal Thoughts, Compassion

TIME: 2 to 3 minutes

Scene One: Lucy and **Amy** *enter from opposite sides.*

Lucy: Hey, Amy! How are you?

Amy: Hey! I'm doing just fine. How about you?

Lucy: Oh, I'm doin' great. How's the English paper coming?

Amy: Oh, it's great. I'm almost done. I can't believe we'll be seniors next year! High school is just flying by.

Lucy: Oh yeah, time goes by really fast. How's Scott?

Amy:	Scott's great. He's staying busy with his job and football, as usual. We're trying to go on a date this weekend so we can spend some time together.
Lucy:	Oh, that sounds great. So are you going to that church dinner on Saturday?
Amy:	Sure! We'll be there!
Lucy:	Great! Well, it was really good seeing you. We should bump into each other more often. Maybe get some coffee sometime and catch up.
Amy:	Yeah, I'd really love that! Please call me.
Lucy:	Will do! Hope to see you soon! *(Both girls begin to exit but then turn around to meet for Scene Two)*

Scene Two: *The same as* **Scene One**, *except this time* **Amy** *pulls out a tissue as if her nose is running, and she talks with a "stuffy" nose.*

Lucy:	Hey, Amy! How are you? *(In this conversation have* **Lucy** *look in different directions at times to show that she's really not paying attention. Nothing too heavy, subtle would be best.)*
Amy:	I'm horrible. I've been really sick with the flu, and I can't seem to shake it. So my English paper is suffering for it. You?
Lucy:	Oh, I'm doin' great. How's the English paper coming?
Amy:	Like I said, I'm having trouble finishing it because I've been so sick. I have to get at least a high B to pass English. My mom is going to kill me if I have to take summer school. She's really counting on me to go to college. I'm not even sure I want to go. I'm so sick of school. Sometimes I wonder what would happen if I just got in my car and drove away and never came back.
Lucy:	Oh yeah, time goes by really fast. How's Scott?
Amy:	I wouldn't really know. You could call his new friend and coworker Kristen and ask her. I'm sure *she* knows all about Scott. He and I haven't seen much of each other lately. I think he's going to break up with me because I won't...you know. I really think he's cheating on me with Kristen.

Lucy: Oh, that sounds great. So are you going to the church dinner on Saturday?

Amy: Oh, I quit going to church a while ago. I can't seem to fit it in anywhere, and I'm so tired all the time. Since my mom and dad's divorce, they don't go to church anymore. So I really don't have anyone to go with. *(Beat)* Lucy, I just feel like my life is spinning out of control, and I really want to get off the ride.

Lucy: Great! Well, it was really good seeing you. We should bump into each other more often. Maybe get some coffee sometime and catch up.

Amy: *(Feeling awkward as if she hasn't been "heard" but tries one last attempt)* Yeah, I'd really love that. *(Imploring)* Please call me.

Lucy: Will do! Hope to see you soon! *(She exits)*

Amy: *(Waits until Lucy is offstage)* You probably won't.

Lights down.

THE END

SKIT 3.5

"THE COAT"

BY TED & NANCIE LOWE, WITH REVISIONS BY TOMMY WOODARD AND EDDIE JAMES

WHAT: As demonstrated in this skit, confusion turns into delight when God's free gift of salvation is accepted.

WHO: Store Owner, Allison (customer)

WHEN: Present Day

WHY: Isaiah 43:1; Luke 19:10; Romans 6:23

WEAR: (COSTUMES AND PROPS) A coat with a label sewn inside it. The Store Owner can wear glasses or an apron.

HOW: This sketch requires the actors to speak immediately after one another. The Store Owner is humble yet confident, while Allison brings the skit to life with energy, enthusiasm, and amazement. The two actors should remain on opposite sides of the stage throughout the skit. The Store Owner's side should be set up as a storefront, whether that's a table with coats on it, a door that he can stand in front of, or other decorations.

THEMES: Salvation, Grace, Shame, Forgiveness

TIME: 5 to 7 minutes

As the scene opens, the **Store Owner** *has his back to the audience while he fiddles around with some items in his store. He then turns around as if he's just noticed the audience.*

Store Owner: Oh, hi! Sorry, I didn't hear you come in. Things are a little slow here today, but welcome to my store. It's very simple: I sell one thing and one thing only—coats.

Allison: I must have passed by that store at least a thousand times, but I never paid that much attention to it. You see, it's on a really busy street with some of my favorite stores that sell lots of my favorite things.

Store Owner:	Every day I see people walk right by my store with lots of bags in their arms and determined looks on their faces. I wonder what's in those bags? What makes them keep coming back again and again? Were the things they bought not good enough, did they not last, or did they just grow tired of them? I would love to ask them sometime, but I have a really hard time getting their attention.
Allison:	One day I was out shopping with my friends, and I asked them if they knew anything about that funny coat store. One said her mother took her there once when she was little. Her mother still loves the store, but my friend thought it was weird. I asked them if they'd go in there with me, you know, just to check things out. No big deal. So we did.
Store Owner:	A few days later, Allison came back. This time she was with a couple of friends, and they even came inside. I thought, "Great, maybe today I could sell three coats." But that didn't happen. I'll never forget the look on Allison's face—she looked excited yet nervous. She liked what I was selling, but her friends didn't. They were giggling and acting all uncomfortable. And the next thing I knew, they just took off laughing. Except for Allison—she just stood there all by herself. And then she looked at me and softly said, "Sorry." Then she dropped her head and left the store too.
Allison:	I was so embarrassed that day, and I'm not even sure why. Was I ashamed of my friends, or was I ashamed that I'd suggested we go into that store? Whatever it was, I felt so uncomfortable. But you know, it wasn't the salesperson's fault, if you could even call him that. I mean, he didn't pressure us or even give us some slick sales pitch. It's as if he believed all those coats were going to sell themselves.
Store Owner:	I thought I'd never see Allison again. But she came back, you know. This time she was all by herself. I told her I had just the coat for her. When I gave it to her, she got "the look." It's the look everybody gets when they take their coat, the one made just for them. They grab it, look inside, and there it is—a label with their name right on it.
Allison:	I couldn't believe it had my name on it. But there it was—right on the label. First of all, how did he know I'd come in the store, much less buy one of his coats? But there it was. The guy said everyone has a coat made just for them. It sounds crazy, I know, but it's true.

Store Owner:	Allison said it was the most beautiful thing she'd ever seen. She asked me how much it costs, and I said, "Allison, this coat is very expensive." She looked discouraged but again she asked, "How much?" And I said…
Allison:	Free. He said it was free! Right after he got through telling me it was expensive, he told me it's free. Then he told me it cost the manufacturer and his son everything just to make that coat for me, and it was made just for me—my free gift.
Store Owner:	When Allison took her coat that day, I was thrilled. But I always hold my breath when someone gets their coat because, believe it or not, some people just don't wear it. They just leave it in the closet or misplace it.
Allison:	I loved that coat. It was the most beautiful, most perfect thing I had ever seen. I even tried to tell people about it. But my parents didn't get it, and my friends just made fun of it. I even tried to tell them how I'd gotten it for free, and they just laughed and said, "Allison, nothing in this world is free!"
Store Owner:	A few days later when I came in to work, Allison was waiting outside the front door of the store.
Allison:	I looked at the salesperson and said, "I'm sorry, but with the life I've led, it doesn't seem fair that I should have this beautiful coat. The voices of my past are telling me that even though it has my name in it, I can't wear it with any kind of integrity. Please give it to someone who deserves it."
Store Owner:	But I told her, "I'm sorry, Allison, there are simply no returns. You see, no one else can wear your coat. It was truly made for you, and the Creator made it fully knowing your past, present, and future. You did nothing to deserve this coat, and you can do nothing to get rid of it. It's time to stop talking about this coat and start wearing it!" *(**Store Owner** puts the coat on **Allison**)*
Allison:	I was finally able to accept my free gift. No looking back in shame.
Store Owner:	*(Out of character, to audience)* The Creator of the universe has made a coat just for you—an everlasting relationship with Jesus Christ.

Allison:	But everyone has a choice. Will I accept the gift or will I allow my friends and situations to prevent me from accepting what God so passionately wants to give me?
Store Owner:	Today, we hope you choose to take the free gift that God has created just for you. God wants to be your warmth, your security, and your salvation, now and forever.
Allison:	In Isaiah 43, God says…
Store Owner:	Don't be afraid because I've saved you…
Allison:	I have called you by name…
Store Owner:	And you are mine.

Lights down.

THE END

MONOLOGUES

INTRO

Why Do I Feel So Alone?

Umm, yeah…maybe that's because you forgot to shower, or because your personality repels people, or maybe…just maybe, it's because you're doing a monologue.

It's been said, "Every church has at least one good actor." And we're the ones who said it—in our first book, *Instant Skits*. (Yes, another shameless plug intended to entice you to purchase it!) But back to monologues. We know you've been there—you've looked over the group of people willing to do a skit, and you can see only one person you trust to "bring home the bacon." Or you've asked for volunteers to do a skit, and only one person showed up. Worse yet, maybe *no one* showed up, and it's just you, baby!

Well, fear no more—we've got monologues for you. Yes, these powerful little "skits for one" are here to help you out when you feel lonely. Monologues are a great way to get a point across because they have the feel of a testimony. There's a unique connection with the audience that comes inherently with a monologue; it's basically one person looking into the eyes of the audience and telling her story. In essence, the audience members become the other characters in the skit. The truth is, you're not alone with a monologue; there's just nobody standing onstage with you. (Hmm, come to think of it, that's pretty much what *alone* means, isn't it?)

Monologues can be one of the most difficult skits to perform. There's such a fine line between grabbing the attention of the audience and overacting. And finding the balance between wandering the stage and utilizing your space is just as tricky. As the only actor, there's no one for you to cue from—and it's all up to you. Talk about pressure! Just think of yourself as the mythic Highlander and tell yourself, "In the end, there can be only *one!*"

Skit Tips:

1. **Who am I, anyway?** The important thing to remember with a monologue is that this is *not* the time to "be yourself." This is the *character's* moment to shine. As with any skit, the actor needs to take on the physical and verbal characteristics of the person he's portraying. Think about how the person would talk, walk, gesture, and even how he would look at the audience. You may be the only actor onstage, but the audience should be watching the *character*, not you.

2. **Don't act like a car salesperson.** Have you ever noticed how the car salespeople on TV overemphasize their gestures and yell at the camera? For some reason, many actors do the same thing with monologues. What makes a monologue easier to watch is when you keep it natural and, if anything, *downplay* all movement and gestures. There is one exception to this rule: If you want to look like Screech from *Saved by the Bell*, then by all means, overdo it.

3. **Get dressed up and propped up.** To help an audience buy into the character you're portraying, monologues are a great opportunity to utilize costumes. Sometimes it could just be a hat or glasses, or you might want to go all out with the full costume regalia. Although many monologues don't require props, some are made more complete with them. Using props also gives the actor something to do with her hands, which just might help her avoid that car-salesperson syndrome we were talking about.

4. **Be still and know that I am acting.** There's something strange and powerful about silence during a monologue. A silent pause at just the right moment can cause an audience to feel uncomfortable, laugh harder, or empathize with the character. In a similar way, making the choice to stay still instead of moving around can sometimes draw focus better than lots of movement. As an actor, don't be afraid to discover the strength of doing what your parents told you to do when you were a kid—"Be quiet and be still!"

5. **Mirror, mirror on the wall, who's the actor with it all?** Before you hit the stage with your monologue, step in front of a mirror and deliver your lines. Even though you'll be the only one onstage, block out any movement you may make. Think about what you're going to do with your hands and facial expressions. We suggest you show your monologue to someone who will be honest with you regarding whether the choices you've made are overdone, boring, or flat.

"DEFINE ME"

BY BEN GAZAWAY, WITH REVISIONS BY TOMMY WOODARD AND EDDIE JAMES

SKIT
4.1

WHAT: A young teenage girl with her whole life in front of her remarks upon the expectations she deals with as she looks to the future.

WHO: Alyssa (14-year-old girl)

WHEN: Present Day

WHY: Proverbs 3:5-6; Matthew 5:48; Luke 6:35

WEAR: Cell phone
(COSTUMES AND PROPS)

HOW: The staging for this monologue is very simple—Alyssa stands center stage with only a cell phone as a prop. As with all monologues, if you have Alyssa move to the left or right, make those movements intentional. If the intent isn't there, it just looks like meandering.

THEMES: Identity, Unconditional Love, Purpose, the Future, Expectations

TIME: 3 to 5 minutes

Alyssa *stands center stage while talking on a cell phone.*

Dad, I know how important those applications are.

She looks at the audience and holds up a finger as if to suggest she'll be with them in a moment.

Yes, I've already filled those out, *(Pause)* **Yes, I put down all the clubs I'm in and all the sports I play.** *(Pause)* **Yes, I've included a picture of Mr. Bungles, but I don't think they really care about my cat.** *(Pause)* **Dad, I'm only a freshman in high school—I don't understand why this can't wait.** *(Pause)* **Okay, we'll talk when I get home. Love you too.**

Alyssa *hangs up the phone.*

(Addressing the audience like a friend) **That was Dad. He's probably looking at bills again and freaking out about how we're going to pay for college. I'm not even old enough to drive a car, and he's already talking about schools and scholarships and grants and financial aid. It gives me a headache just thinking about it.**

She pauses and motions with her cell phone.

Have you ever felt like your life has been defined and you never really got a say in it? I mean, take Dad, for example. He's decided that I'm going to be the first doctor in the family. He'll say things like *(In her best "Dad" voice)*, **"Think of all the good you can do for people when you're a doctor," and "It'll take better grades than that to get into med school." I've told him I don't do needles and I don't do blood. I passed out last year when we dissected frogs in biology! He's determined, though.**

Now my aunt Monica has decided I'm going to be an engineer just like her. She's always like, "Sweetie, being good at math always pays." I'm like, "Look, I'm good at numbers, and I'm good at letters, but I can't do numbers *and* letters!" She won't hear of it, though. Last year, she gave me a calculator for my birthday. Who gives a 14-year-old girl a calculator for her birthday? No hidden agenda there or anything.

My friends are just as bad. They're always like *(Impersonating a teenage girl)*, **"OMG, girl! You are the best singer *ever*…you're going to be like a rock star and have your own show on the Disney Channel with cute vampire boys and stuff!" I tell them that with three brothers, the last thing I need is more blood-sucking boys in my life.**

Oh, and my coach is always telling me how if I can just grow another four inches, I'll be a starter by my sophomore year. Thanks, Coach, I'll get right on that.

The truth is, I don't know if I *want* to be a doctor or an engineer or a rock star or some star athlete. But I can't tell *them* that. It's like I've been reduced to a word in a dictionary, and everyone else gets to fill in the definition.

Don't get me wrong—I know they all love me. *(Pause)* **But sometimes it feels like they love *their* versions of me more than they love the real me. It's transactional…conditional…** *(Pause)*

This may sound kinda corny, but I take comfort knowing that Jesus went through the same thing. Now, he didn't have folks wanting him to be an engineer or a star athlete, but lots of people wanted him to fit into their molds. You see, to some people, Jesus was a "good teacher" or a prophet or a political leader. *(Pause)* **It was like no one wanted the real Jesus…they only wanted the Jesus they liked. Everybody had their own ideas of who he should be.**

But Jesus was and is bigger than their tiny definitions. He found his identity in the words of a heavenly Father who said: "You are my Son, whom I love; with you I am well pleased."

Because of this truth, *my* identity is found not in the clothes I wear or the music I listen to or my hobbies or occupation. I am *more* than the sum of all these parts. I am a child of the King of Kings, and *he* alone has the power to define me.

(Pause, then look out at the audience) **What about you?**

THE END

SKIT 42

"DYLAN GOES TO CHURCH"

BY MELINDA WHITTEN, WITH REVISIONS BY TOMMY WOODARD AND EDDIE JAMES

WHAT: A look inside the heart of a young man named Dylan whose life was drastically changed thanks to the love of Jesus that was shown to him.

WHO: Dylan (male teenager or young adult)

WHEN: Present Day

WHY: Matthew 9:13; Luke 15:7; Ephesians 1:7

WEAR: Jacket, glasses, fake tattoos, shirt with the initials "DM"
(COSTUMES AND PROPS)

HOW: The actor begins by speaking to the audience as though introducing a guest speaker. He then transforms into Dylan, a new believer who's led a very different life from those sitting in the audience. To accomplish this transformation, include clothing that can be added or removed, such as a jacket or glasses. The Dylan character must wear a shirt with the initials "DM" clearly portrayed. For added effect, most theater-supply stores carry fake tattoos that can be revealed during the transformation.

THEMES: Grace, Forgiveness, Love, Acceptance, New Identity

TIME: 5 minutes

A young man stands alone onstage.

Sometimes, we're guilty of doing nothing because we think, "What difference can I make?" I want to help answer that question. I want to introduce you to someone who was once a visitor to the youth group. He's what I like to call the "extreme visitor." Some of you may have met our speaker already—he's pretty hard to miss.

Actor *slowly begins the transformation into* **Dylan.**

But you know him, or you know a kid like him. He's the kid who dresses differently—you know, the one with the crazy hair? He's the dude standing alone in the corner...quiet. But when he does speak, every sentence is punctuated with a four-letter word. And he knows them all.

Or he might be the kid who has no clue what "personal space" means—he totally pops that protective bubble and gets right up in your face with spit flying from his mouth 'cause he's talking about his, his, collection of mutant zombie transformers or whatever. And he's hard to shake off, and you think, "Why did I say hi?"

But you did say hi, and you saved a seat for him. Some of you invited him to your small group and a movie afterward. And a few of you—those gifted with patience—really listened to him. You listened about mutant zombie transformers or the exhaust system on a souped-up race car. And you listened to his story—an uncomfortable story so totally different from yours.

Save the last piece of the transformation until **Dylan** *says his name. Maybe it's putting on the glasses or pulling up the hood of a sweatshirt. The actor might also change his posture or shove his hands into his pockets to help communicate the transformation from host into* **Dylan***.*

So I'd like to introduce... *(Actor puts on glasses and takes on the physical characteristics of* **Dylan***)* Dylan Marlowe. *(Points to the large "DM" on his shirt)* **My name is Dylan Marlowe—just in case you zone out like when** *(Insert your own youth pastor's name)* **goes on forever.**

"DM" means something else to me though, 'cause I don't feel like the dude that I was on the streets with the booze and the bongs. And I was so freakin' stoked to talk to you guys... *(Pauses and looks offstage or toward youth pastor)* **Oh crap,** *(Note: Make sure it's okay to utter the words "crap" and "freakin'." We realize some churches and denominations don't see these as bad words and others would frown upon them pretty heavily. Use good judgment and get wisdom before adding or deleting.)* **can I say freakin'?** *(To audience)* **My grandma has this jar, and she makes me pay a quarter every time I cuss—flippin' filled the thing first day I moved back in with her. She's got all these lame words on her list, and I'm like, "Nana, poser is not a bad word." But if she ain't heard it, you got to quarter up. And if you argue about it, it's 50 cents.** *(Dylan points to someone in the audience)* **Isn't that right, Hunter? Hunter came over and told Nana he brought his Wii.** *(Back to Hunter)* **What'd she make you pay? Like five bucks or something?**

Nana's a pain in the... *(Pause)* **I almost used a two-dollar word there. Anyway, she's a pain. But she loves me, and she took me back when I was screwed up.** *(Pause)* **See, my mom took off when I was 11 'cause Nana wouldn't give her any more money for drugs. I took off from Nana when I was 14. I hated Nana's stupid rules and all her spiritual shh** *(Catching himself)* **...stuff.**

She didn't want me to turn out like Mom, but…I did, sort of. I was an alcoholic by the time I was 14. I was living on the streets by 15. I spent my first night in jail on my 16th birthday. Happy birthday to me.

So what changed? Well, I was broke. Had the shakes 'cause I couldn't manage to steal nothin' to get a bottle. I couldn't even beg 'cause no one would make eye contact, you know? You ought to see how fast people can move when someone like me is around. They're like Nana's cat, you know, all calm and talking on their phones, and then they spot the SHK—stinky homeless kid—and it's—(Slaps hands together) "Oh crud, I gotta cross the street." They thought I was worthless. I knew I was. I mean, Mom didn't want me, right? Dad took off before I was born.

Somehow I wind up walking down this street in Nana's neighborhood. I don't know how I wound up there—guess my feet just went someplace familiar. If you ask my Nana, she'll say it was God. (Shrugging) All I know is that I was done. Broke, sick, starving, wandering the streets. And when my feet finally stopped moving, I looked up and saw I was in front of Nana's house.

I asked Nana if I could stay a night. She said I could stay forever. (Dylan points to the initials DM on his shirt) "Difference Made." Nana helped me sober up. She says that first week she learned a lot of words she'd never heard before. That's when the quarter jar was born. I asked her if she was playing the slots with my money. She didn't laugh.

After a while Nana started bugging me about coming here to church. I told her, "Nana, I don't have enough quarters for two jars. And besides, God wouldn't want me." She looked sad, but I knew all the crazy stuff I'd done. I knew church people, too. They were the same people who crossed the street so I wouldn't stink 'em up, you know?

But Nana is…stubborn. Our dinner prayers got stinkin' long, like "I'm gonna starve before the Amen" long. (Dylan bows head and clasps hands) "Dear Lord, thank you for your provision and this wonderful meal. Thank you for the return of my precious grandson and his healing. Open his heart to you, Lord, so that he may know your amazing love, grace, and forgiveness of his many, many…many, (Dylan opens one eye, closes it, and continues) many sins. Draw him back to you and to church so he can surround himself in your love and in the love of others. Amen."

(Dylan looks up and smiles) Dude, she wore me down. By the end of the week, I struck a deal. I'd try church if she'd keep her prayers short—as in less than five minutes.

So I came. Didn't think anything would come of it. I knew you guys would take one look at me, (Tugs at his shirt) my Goodwill clothes, my marked-up arms, my scars inside and out, and think…worthless.

(Looking out at the audience as though singling someone out) **But you,** *(He points)* **you came right up to me. I thought, "Crud, I didn't even make it in the door, and they're gonna toss me out on my butt. Nana's gonna kill me." But you shook my hand and pulled me over to meet your best friend.** *(This is emotional for **Dylan**, hard for him to say)* **I waited to see if you'd wipe your hand on your jeans, you know, like I was dirt. You didn't.** *(Pointing to the initials)* **Difference Made.**

(Pointing to someone else) **You brought over a box of doughnuts, and when you found out we went to the same school, you asked if I wanted to catch the game on Friday.** *(Pointing to the initials)* **Difference Made.**

(Nodding in another direction) **And when I broke down crying at the retreat because I knew this Jesus you guys were so stoked about would never love me and my totally screwed-up past, you didn't freak out.** *(Motioning to someone else)* **Well,** *you* **freaked out a little. But hey, it's totally understandable when some big dude starts crying. You got over it…and I found forgiveness. I found Jesus because…you guys saw more than lame clothes or crazy hair or bad language…family life, weirdness, or whatever shh…stuff that makes someone different.**

What difference can you make? My name is Dylan Marlowe, and I'm a new believer. *(Pointing to his shirt)* **Difference Made.**

THE END

SKIT 4.3

"THE BOW TIE"

BY TED & NANCIE LOWE, WITH REVISIONS BY TOMMY WOODARD AND EDDIE JAMES

WHAT: A young man, just moments before his wedding, shares some insight about his previous choices and how they've affected this day.

WHO: Robby

WHEN: Present Day

WHY: 1 Corinthians 6:18; Hebrews 13:4; 1 Thessalonians 4:4

WEAR:
(COSTUMES AND PROPS) A child-size Sunday school chair, a standing mirror that Robby (dressed as a groom) can look into as he tries to put on an untied bow tie

HOW: This monologue can be done while Robby works on his tie while looking in the mirror, stopping now and then to talk to the audience. Keep a good pace and even time this monologue beforehand so it doesn't feel long. Obviously, because of the subject matter, make sure the actor looks believable as a groom. Giggles from the crowd are the last things you want.

THEMES: Love, Sex, Marriage, Choices, Consequences

TIME: 6 to 7 minutes

The scene opens as **Robby** *prepares for his wedding in a children's Sunday school room at a church. He's already made several unsuccessful attempts at tying his bow tie.*

Come in. You got here just in time. I can't seem to get this dumb thing tied. Bow ties. Who wears bow ties besides Orville Redenbacher and maybe Colonel Sanders? No one, that's who. Apparently grooms, popcorn icons, and fried chicken magnates are the only ones who wear these stupid things. I've tried everything. I've tried to tie it like a shoelace, and that looks even more like a bow. I've tried tying it like a lasso, and I couldn't get enough slack. Maybe I should try tying it like a noose. Yeah, that's it. *(Laughs uncomfortably)*

Big weddings. I don't know what all the fuss is about anyway. My friend and his fiancée got married in Jamaica. All they had to do was show up in their bathing suits, and a reggae priest

wearing Rasta beads legalized it, "Mon." But oh no, not my Jill. She'd have nothing less than a big wedding with all the trimmings. So here I am, stuck in the five-year-olds' Sunday school classroom, sweating bullets and scared to death. To be honest with you, it's not just the bow tie I'm worried about. I'm worried about tonight. You know, the big wedding night.

Oh, it's not what you think. You see, I've never been around anyone like Jill. She's incredibly funny, she's beautiful, and she's the smartest person I know. I'd rather be with her than anyone. She loves God, and we decided to wait to have sex until we got married. You may be thinking, *Oh, you're inexperienced! That's why you're so nervous.* No. I'm nervous because…I AM experienced.

Since as early as I can remember, "sex" is what all the guys teased and talked about. Anything that could be turned into something sexual usually was. Even as a really young guy, I was so curious about sex. As early as junior high, I started hearing rumors around school that this guy and this girl got together. I wanted to be like those people. I wanted to be the one everyone was talking about. Let's be honest—I wanted to have sex. So I got my chance. I wasn't even 15 yet. I couldn't even drive a car. But one night, after a football game, I left with a girl I barely knew. Her parents were out of town, so we went to her house and…well, you know… we had sex.

Afterward I felt a million different things all at once. I was excited to tell my friends, I was confused, I was proud of myself, I was ashamed of myself. Through all the feelings, I knew one thing for sure: I wanted to go home. I wanted to get away from this girl. I know it sounds mean, but it's true. I just wanted to go home. Once I got home, I immediately called every guy I knew and said I should now be referred to as "Stallion." I was now known as an experienced manly man of the world. This began my quest to search and conquer. My friends and I exchanged stories of all our conquests. No one was really listening to each other, though. We were just thinking of ways to make ourselves seem like more of a conqueror than the other guy.

But when we got girlfriends, it was different. You know, we showed them more respect. You didn't share your intimate stories with everyone—just *almost* everyone. I'm kidding. Girlfriends were different. I was more committed. More committed to telling them what they wanted to hear to get them to sleep with me. Then there was college where we were all "adults." There seemed to be more serious relationships, but there also seemed to be a lot of serious cheating.

My friends and I still laughed and talked about our victories on the sex field. While it seemed everyone was having sex—and I could justify it that way—I knew deep down it was wrong. Well, maybe it wasn't so deep down. I knew it was wrong. So here I am today, preparing to marry the woman I love, and I'm scared. You know, I once heard about "sexual ghosts"—memories of the people you've slept with—how they float through your mind while you're in bed with your spouse. I don't know if it's just a myth to scare people into virginity, or if it's the honest truth. But tonight I'm going to find out. Man, I hope it's not true.

Tonight, I will treat Jill the way God wants me to. By choosing God's plan this time, I will experience sex the way God intended—a true expression of love within the commitment to my wife and to God. And in some beautifully mysterious way, the Bible says Jill and I will become one. I honestly don't see how that's possible—you see, I never really became one with the other girls I had sex with. Somehow, I have to figure out how to change my perceptions about sex—to take something I've viewed as a way to conquer a woman and turn it into a way to love a woman. *(Pause, as if taking in the magnitude of the task before him)*

This is going to take some time. But with God's grace and Jill's help, I know it's possible.

Well, I guess I'd better stop talking and learn how to tie this dumb bow tie. After all, today is the big day. And tonight is… *(More sadly than excited)* the big night.

THE END

"WHAT NOW?"

BY EDDIE JAMES AND JOHNNY BAKER

WHAT: A teenage girl has to face the consequences after having sex with her boyfriend.

WHO: Jill

WHEN: Present Day

WHY: 1 Corinthians 6:18; Hebrews 13:4; 1 Thessalonians 4:4

WEAR:
(COSTUMES
AND PROPS)   Jill should be dressed as a regular teenager.

HOW: This sketch can be very powerful if the actress truly knows her lines and is able to deliver them with confidence and sincerity. The correct tone and expression are critical for this sketch to be interesting and understandable, but the impact makes it worth the effort.

THEMES: Love, Sex, Choices, Consequences, Responsibility, Abstinence, Parents

TIME: 5 minutes

As the scene opens, **Jill***, enters the stage; she's about to give her testimony of what's going on her life.*

(Clearly she has some heavy things on her heart) **Hey. My name is Jill. I'm sixteen years old. I've been going out with this guy . . . who will remain nameless . . . for quite a while. Major commitment. Very serious.** *(as if answering a question from audience)* **How long? About five months. You may say that isn't a long time, but for me it seems like an eternity. It's the longest I've ever been with a guy.**

You see, I love him. *(Doubting)* **I *think* I love . . . no, no, I do. This is love. It has to be, right? I've never felt like this about someone. See, the reason I know I love him is, well,** *(Pause)* **we, we have . . . you know . . .** *(Beat)* **. . . a lot.**

We have been having, um, "relations" . . . oh, you know what I mean . . . for a while now. *(Beat)* About two months and four days—but who's counting?

This might sound kind of weird, but I'm kind of getting tired of it. Crazy, right? I mean we're always sneaking around, lying to our parents, and to be honest I've never been with anyone before, and I'm not sure if I'm even doing things right.

I live in constant fear of his parents finding out. They would freak out if they knew what we were up to when we go out on dates. They don't like me anyway. His dad is a big wheel at his church. I'm not that religious or anything. It makes for very uncomfortable silent conversations when he picks me up.

My mom used to go to church. She would take me and my sister with her. She doesn't go anymore. I think it's 'cause Dad always gave her a hard time about being weak minded and taking religion too seriously or something.

Anyway, what's been bugging me lately is when I used to go to church, I remember there being a big deal about waiting 'til you're married before you . . . My parents didn't wait. I guess you could say I was an "oops" baby. Even though Mom says I wasn't a mistake. So I've got all this guilt now. I keep thinking my parents would be happier if I'd never been born.

And then I go to my boyfriend's church, and what do you know? They're talking all about keeping yourself for your future mate and all this kind of stuff. I don't know how he does it. I'm sitting there sweating, feeling like I have a big sign on my forehead that says, "Yes, we're doing it!" He's got everyone fooled into thinking he's waiting.

When I get away from it I think these are just scare tactics from the church. 'Cause how could the feelings I feel for him be wrong? How can they judge whether or not we're in love or not?

That's not even the whole problem. I don't want to say that I'm being pressured into having sex, but sometimes I think that if I don't, or say no...he'll lose interest in me. So I always say yes.

Except now there's something else. I had the "symptoms." You know what I mean?

I called him two days ago and told him I'm late. I told him not to worry, that it's just a normal thing. I had a friend buy me a kit. But for the last two days I'd been worrying, playing out all these scenes in my mind. I'd been praying that I'm only late and nothing else. I mean, we were careful . . . weren't we?

Today I got the results. *(Beat)* I'm, um . . . I'm *(Pause; to the point of tears)* I never wanted to do what my parents did to me. I didn't want this. I'm too young for this. I'm not ready to be a mom. *(Beat) (To audience)* What now?

THE END

"THE WEIRD KID"

BY REBECCA WIMMER, WITH REVISIONS BY TOMMY WOODARD AND EDDIE JAMES

WHAT: A boy who's been labeled "The Weird Kid" gives us an inside look into what he's really thinking and feeling.

WHO: Male Teenager

WHEN: Present Day

WHY: Psalm 10:14; 25:16; Jeremiah 30:17

WEAR:
(COSTUMES AND PROPS) The actor should be dressed in stereotypical and alienating clothes (i.e., black and unfashionable, black nail polish, etc.).

HOW: This script is best performed by a strong male teenager. His posture should be slouchy and his demeanor cool, quiet, and mysterious. It would be very easy to overplay it or be melodramatic, so be very careful to remain true to the character. People need to be drawn to the character and his heart, not to the acting.

THEMES: Loneliness, Outcast, Friendship, Reaching Out, Popularity, Rejection

TIME: 4 to 5 minutes

What are you waiting for? For me to say something? Am I supposed to tell you something about myself? Haven't you already figured out who I am? I know people see me. They know things about me...or at least they think they do. I'm the weird kid. The one who sits alone. Eats alone. Walks alone. Is alone.

I'm the weird kid your youth director always encourages you to talk to. Be kind to. Not dismiss. And every Sunday night you think...*I could do that.* Be nice to the weird kid. But Monday comes, and you pass by my locker, you see me sitting by myself, you sit right beside me in math class, you watch the punks pick on me, and you do what? The same thing you did last Monday, and the same thing you'll do tomorrow and the next day and the next.

Yeah. I know who you are. You walk around school wearing your little Christian T-shirts. You invite all the "normal" kids to go on your retreat, to your Sunday night thing, your small group, your road trip. You befriend the popular people, and they like you and think you're cool enough.

Yeah. I know you. And you're just like them. You might not push me into my locker or threaten to beat me up, but you certainly aren't helping anything. But I don't need your help. I'm not some project. I'm not a makeover show waiting to happen. I'm just a kid. Like you. And maybe I'm going through a rough time. Maybe my home isn't as clean, as big, and as safe as yours. Maybe my mom's a drunk, and my dad left—or maybe they're just like your parents and just like you. I think they're lame. Maybe I'm adopted. Maybe my grandparents are raising me. Maybe my wrists have scars or my dog died. Maybe I'm just shy or confused or scared or afraid or lonely.

But maybe we like the same movies. Play the same games. Have the same posters hanging in our rooms. Maybe we laugh at the same jokes. Watch the same shows. Play the same songs when we're really sad. Maybe I'm the best friend you'll never have.

Yeah, you've heard a lot of things about me, and some of it might be true. All of it might be true. None of it might be true. But you wouldn't know that because you haven't asked.

Every Sunday night you think, *This time I'll do it. I'll talk to the weird kid. Invite the weird kid. Smile at the weird kid.* And every Monday…nothing. *(Pause as he remembers)* No, wait. I remember now. You said hi to me once. It was a Wednesday right before school got out. I was walking out of Spanish class. You said hi when you passed me.

Why did you do that? Why do I remember that? Did it matter to me?

Maybe I felt…seen. Maybe in that moment I didn't feel alone. Maybe I felt something other than worthless. Maybe just then I didn't feel like the weird kid. *(He snaps out of it)*

Well, whatever. I don't need you to do or say anything. You can just be like everyone else come Monday. I mean, just because you go to church…that shouldn't really make you any different…should it? I wouldn't really know…no one has ever taken the time to tell me.

So what if Jesus loves me? That doesn't mean you have to…does it? After all, I'm just the weird kid.

Lights down.

THE END

DUETS AND ENSEMBLES

INTRO

Do You Like My Ensemble?

In the same way a clothing "ensemble" is several pieces that together make a great outfit, an acting ensemble is several actors who together create a great skit. Just make sure you don't try to wear cutoffs with a jacket and tie!

An ensemble can be great because it paints the picture rather than tells the story (as in a monologue). However, ensembles can be a train wreck if you don't plan and rehearse enough. To ease you into ensembles, we've chosen five primarily comedic scripts to which you can add more actors as extras.

One of the best clothing ensembles is a simple T-shirt and jeans. Likewise, a duet is a simple ensemble that's a great way to ease into bigger and better things. In this section of the book, you'll find duets to get you started and ensembles that can help you add more people when you're ready.

Speaking of getting more people involved, check out *Skit Training 101* for some great tips on how to identify your team members' gifts and talents and help them get involved as writers, directors, prop people, lighting and sound techs, etc.

Skit Tips:

1. **"P" is for pacing.** Ensembles are the hardest to pull off. Do you have enough mics? Is the stage big enough? Do you have enough time? Look at big-cast TV shows; if there are six people in a crowded space, they had to make it look simple. Start with a small ensemble, otherwise known as a "duet." Duets provide the benefits of ensemble skits with the ease of working with just two people. Get your chops around the duets first and then go for the ensembles. Chemistry is very important

with duets and ensembles...don't be afraid to try different actors in these roles for the right mix.

2. **"P" is for projection.** Although projection is important in all the types of skits in this book, it's most important in ensemble pieces. Why? Because rarely do you find a venue or stage with enough wireless microphones for everyone involved. Therefore, it's important to make sure your actors can be heard and understood. If one person isn't heard in your ensemble, then the entire skit can be lost. That's a lot of pressure for your "mumbler" kids.

3. **"P" is for placement.** Staging is crucial in an ensemble piece. First, make sure you have ample room to perform. Then block your piece so everyone can be seen and heard all throughout the skit. Take the time to move people around and find the best spots for them to stand so they don't have to turn their backs to the audience. It can get crowded very quickly in an ensemble piece, if you're not careful. And for goodness' sake, try to be creative—don't make your actors stand in a straight line. Utilize different levels, such as having some actors positioned on furniture, some sitting on the ground, and some standing.

4. **"P" is for props.** Frequently in an ensemble piece, the actors will need to hand things to each other. Make sure you've secured your props far enough in advance to allow your actors a few rehearsals with these items. Also, if you're pantomiming your objects instead of using actual props, it's easy for the skit to slide toward "corny." So have your actors practice with their imaginary props to make sure they're conveying the items accurately.

5. **"P" is for paying attention.** With multiple people on the stage and multiple things going on, it's very easy for actors to lose their place or forget their lines. So listen up, actors—the key is to *pay attention* to what's going on. Listen to each other. Interact like your characters would. If you're offstage, don't goof off. Stand in the wings and watch what's going on. And always be prepared to step back onstage. It's so tempting to drop character while you're not the focus of the action. So keep this in mind—"If you're *on*, then you're *in*." Simply stated, this means that if you're somewhere on the stage, then you're still in character. No exceptions. So pay attention, or your whole group will pay for it.

6. **"P" is for costumes.** Yeah, yeah, we know. But what did you want us to say? "P" is for "Play Clothes?" (Darn, you're right—that would have worked.) Anyway, costumes can play a big role in helping your audience buy into your ensemble skit. The more people you have onstage, the easier it is for your audience to get lost in knowing who's who. Even if your costuming is simple and small, do something to help differentiate between the characters.

7. **"C" is for cookie.** And folks, that's good enough for me.

DUETS

"BELONGING TO HIM"

BY SARAH WALL, WITH REVISIONS BY TOMMY WOODARD AND EDDIE
JAMES

WHAT: Two teenage girls discuss their very different concepts of love.

WHO: Sam, Bree

WHEN: Present Day

WHY: Proverbs 14:12; Romans 1:22-25; 1 John 5:21

WEAR:
(COSTUMES
AND PROPS)
The two female actors should be dressed as typical teenage girls hanging out in a typical teenage room. Also needed are two cell phones, schoolbooks, a notebook and pencil, a pillow, and a pile of clothes next to Bree.

HOW: The sketch takes place in Sam's room, with Sam standing and narrating to the audience during the opening. Bree is busy texting on her cell phone and addressing Sam, not the audience.

THEMES: Relationships, Dating, Love, Witnessing, Friendship

TIME: 10 minutes

Scene opens with **Bree** *doing homework in* **Sam's** *bedroom and talking to* **Sam** *at the same time.* **Sam** *is addressing the audience. The first part is "two different worlds" at the same time:* **Bree** *is texting on her phone and talking to* **Sam***, while* **Sam** *is talking to the audience as the set-up.*

Sam: So I've got this friend.

Bree: Hey, you wanna go see a movie on Friday or something?

Sam: Her name's Bree.

Bree: Oooh! I think *(Name a current "chick flick")* is supposed to be opening this weekend!

Sam:	She's pretty cool, super nice…
Bree:	Hey, I meant to tell you that color looks really good on you.
Sam:	…honest to a fault…
Bree:	Sam, NO JOKE, your running shoes smell like some creature that ate broccoli and cabbage crawled up in 'em and died. *(She looks up long enough from her cell phone to try to identify the location of the shoes, then puts down her phone and goes back to doing her homework)*
Sam:	…but I always know she cares about me.
Bree:	I still love you, though.
Sam:	Even when we totally disagree.
Bree:	I think people should run only if they're being chased by wild dogs.
Sam:	She CAN be a bit predictable at times.
Bree:	Hey, what are you doing tonight?
Sam:	ESPECIALLY when it comes to the God stuff.
Bree:	I have a bunch of friends who wanna meet you.
Sam:	She brings that up a lot, actually.
Bree:	'Cuz you know what I was thinking?
Sam:	Here's the part where she invites me to her church…in 5, 4, 3, 2…
Bree:	*(Looks up from her studies)* It'd be pretty cool if you'd come with me to youth group tonight.

Sam *now turns to* **Bree** *and engages in the conversation, rather than addressing the audience. She begins looking through the piles of clothes around the set.*

Sam:	Yeah…I'll totally come visit with you…one day.
Bree:	*(Playfully)* Ha ha! Wow. Seriously, Sam, if you were any less enthused, you'd be in a coma. Look at you! You look like a kid being dragged to the dentist on her birthday!

Sam: What are you talking about? I mean it. I'll definitely go hang out with you and your Jesus friends on Wednesday. Or whenever it is you do your…you know…religious stuff.

Bree: *(Smiles)* Now I KNOW we've had this conversation before…

Sam: Okay, fine, I take it back. I didn't mean "religious"…

Bree: …you KNOW the last thing in the world I wanna do is make you "religious."

Sam: *(Sighs)* Yes, Bree, I know. *(Distracted by her clothing options, she holds up two choices)* Hey, help me…which one do you think is cuter—this one or this one?

Bree: Umm, definitely THAT one. *(She points to the more modest option of the two)*

Sam: *(Scowls a bit)* I should have known you'd say that.

Bree: Why? What's this for, anyway?

Sam: *(Smiles wryly)* Well…I have a date tonight.

Bree: Oh yeah, with who?

Sam: Ben.

Bree: Ben Phelps?!

Sam: Yeah, Ben Phelps. Why are you looking at me like that?

Bree: Well, I guess I've just observed a certain…uh…pattern in his "dating" habits.

Sam: Bree, you're about as subtle as Christy Perkins' red leather pants.

Bree: You asked! *(Playfully throws a pillow at **Sam**)*

Sam: *(Lightheartedly bats the pillow away)* Hey, watch it! I'm concentrating here!

Bree: I can see that. *(Pause)* Tell you what—I'll dress you for your date. *(She starts sifting through the clothes)* Got anything flannel? Maybe a nice turtleneck and sweatpants?

Sam: Ha! Yeah right! Flannel and sweatpants don't exactly fit the...uh...look I'm going for.

Bree: Oh, but this does? *(She holds up the immodest outfit that **Sam** held up earlier)* Sam, exactly what look are you aiming for? "Hypothermia Chic"?

Sam: *(Grabs clothes)* Oh, you're crazy!

Bree: I'm not kidding! The only way you could wear less material is if you glued on a couple of Post-It Notes™ and called it a "skirt."

Sam: *(Sarcastically)* Oh, you're a truckload of funny. We'll see who's got jokes when I'M the one with a date for the dance in three weeks.

Bree: I'm more worried about you and what's gonna happen before that three weeks is up. What's so great about Ben, anyway? Sometimes he acts like he doesn't even know you when we're at school.

Sam: I know you won't get this, but he's actually nice to me when we're alone.

Bree: And that's okay with you?

Sam: Whatever. It's been too long since I've had a boyfriend. *(Changes the subject)* Anyway...so what do you normally do when you hang out with your church friends? Hold hands and sing "Jesus Loves Me"? Brainstorm creative ways to avoid fun of any sort?

Bree: *(Laughs)* Yeah, something like that. No, mostly we hang out. Talk. Look at what God has to say in the Bible. Stuff like that.

Sam: No offense, Bree, but NONE of that is gonna find me a boyfriend.

Bree: Would that be SO horrible? What's wrong with being single for a while?

Sam: No way. I'm just not that kind of person. Don't get me wrong: I agree there's a God and all. But God's not gonna want to hang out on Friday nights. And my guess is that God's not gonna rent a tux to match my dress for the dance.

Bree: Look, I understand the appeal of having a boyfriend. And I'm not saying you're wrong for wanting a relationship. I just...

Sam:	Just what?
Bree:	*(Pauses)* Sam, do you REALLY, honestly believe that having a boyfriend is the most important thing, ever?
Sam:	No, obviously, it's not the most important thing EVER, but…Bree, if the guys around us don't want us…I mean, what does that say about me? I refuse to be the girl who couldn't get a date. Not even if she watched him play XBox® Live and eat pizza every day for the rest of his life.
Bree:	Okay, but what's the cost? What are you willing to trade for having a guy around all the time?
Sam:	It's not like that.
Bree:	Well, explain it to me then. Because obviously you're not going out with Ben because he treats you like a queen. And it's probably safe to say you're not dressing like this to highlight your dazzling personality. *(Holds up immodest outfit)*
Sam:	Look, Ben may not have a lot to say to me when other people are around. But when we're alone, he says the sweetest things. Bree, he thinks I'm really pretty. He tells me all the time. And when he says things like that…well…I don't mind doing things that make him happy because he makes me feel good about myself.
Bree:	*(Slightly under her breath)*…trading the truth for a lie…
Sam:	What was that?
Bree:	No, it's just…it's just that I wish you'd GET it…
Sam:	I know what it takes to GET a guy's attention and that's what I plan on doing.
Bree:	Yeah, but Sam, it's ALL a lie!
Sam:	Ugh, what in the world are you talking about? Ben really does think I'm pretty…
Bree:	No, I mean…like buying the lie that we're only worth the number of guys who wanna use us. Like we should settle for the cheap "I love you" and then just bandage a bruised heart EVERY TIME he moves on

to another girl. *Those* lies.

Sam: You know, you talk about "lies," but this is what works.

Bree: The thing about lies, Sam...they make a lot of promises, but in the end they can't deliver.

Sam: Well, that's great and all, but...*(Pauses for a moment, processing)* what if I'm not entirely sure what the truth even is?

Bree: Well, I'd tell you that I *do* know what the truth is and that you can know it too. But I don't know a new way to say it so you'll actually hear me.

Sam: *(Trying to joke)* Whoa! Is Bree Anderson actually giving up on something? You never give up! I'm a little hurt. Come on, Bree, don't give up on me!

Bree: Okay, what if I told you I know Someone who can help you with knowing the truth? *(Holds out her phone)* Would that make you call Ben and reschedule?

Sam: *(Takes phone somewhat reluctantly)* Probably not. But I'll think about it.

Bree: Okay, it's your call. But if you do decide to go on this date, promise me one thing?

Sam: I guess I can. What is it?

Bree: Promise me you'll wear those running shoes, and then I won't have to worry about ANYONE coming within 37 feet of you. *(Throws a handful of clothes at **Sam**, the girls share a laugh)* Hey, you got anything to eat around here? I'm starved.

Sam: *(Distracted, staring down at the phone in her hand)* Huh? Oh, uh yeah, there's stuff in the kitchen downstairs. Go grab something. I'll be right down. I'm just going to clean up some of this. *(Puts the phone down, starts folding clothes)*

Bree: All right, sounds good. *(**Bree** exits)*

Sam glances back at the phone as she folds clothes, seemingly resolved not to pick it up. Her cleaning slows again as she reconsiders, eventually stopping what she's doing, picking *up the phone, and sitting down on a chair or bed. She looks at the phone again, then up to the ceiling as she thinks, and then back to the phone again. She slowly dials and lifts the phone to her ear. After a pause, she speaks.*

Sam: Hey Ben, it's me. *(Pause)* Sam. *(Another pause)* No…SAMANTHA! *(Visibly upset that he doesn't recognize her, but she recovers quickly)* Aw, I guess I can't stay mad when you talk to me like that. *(Pauses to listen)* Funny you should ask. I was actually calling to talk to you about tonight…

Lights down.

THE END

"FORGIVE ME?"

BY TED & NANCIE LOWE, WITH REVISIONS BY TOMMY WOODARD AND EDDIE JAMES

WHAT: A brother and sister demonstrate the importance of forgiveness.

WHO: Samantha, Jeff

WHEN: Present Day

WHY: Matthew 5:23-24; Luke 6:37

WEAR:
(COSTUMES AND PROPS) Cell phones, a stuffed bear that's been fixed so its head will rip off during a struggle, three chairs

HOW: The expressions and timing of this skit are extremely important. The characters are interacting with an imaginary counselor, so employ natural pauses where the counselor would be speaking. Also, the flashback scenes can be done two ways:

Film all the flashbacks with your original actors and show the scenes on video in the appropriate spots during the script.

Have another pair of actors, dressed identically to the first set, stand on the other side of the stage to act out the flashbacks. If this approach is chosen, the primary pair of actors should freeze during the flashback scenes.

THEMES: Forgiveness, Bitterness, Family, Grace

TIME: 10 to 12 minutes

Scene One: Jeff and **Samantha** *are waiting in the counselor's office, seated in chairs. Leave one empty chair for the counselor who will "enter" during this scene.*

Jeff: *(Arms folded, fidgeting with his feet)* I can't believe you got us into this, Samantha.

Samantha: I got us into this? You're the one who's always running to Mom and

	Dad.
Jeff:	Yeah, because you're always driving me crazy.
Samantha:	Oh, that's funny. I'm driving YOU crazy. You're the one who's always taking my _____ *(Name some electronic device)* without asking, reading my emails, responding to my texts with things I'd never say, and listening to my phone calls.
Jeff:	I don't listen in on your *(Mockingly)* "phone conversations." *(Pause, then in a feminine voice)* "Oh, Katherine, don't you think Kyle Jackson is a real hottie?"
Samantha:	*(Slaps his arm)* Why you little…I get no privacy. I wish I *were* Katherine. She's an only child. Then I wouldn't even be at this stupid counselor's office.
Jeff:	Whoa, whoa, whoa—I'm the one who's supposed to be the only child, here. I don't know if Mom and Dad have broken it to you yet, but someone dropped you off on our doorstep…*(Pause)* 'cause you were so ugly.
Samantha:	You are such an annoying little jerk.
Jeff:	*I'm* annoying? Miss "Live in the Bathroom Until the Year 2021"? *(Actor should always name a date 10 years from the current date)*
Samantha:	Can I help it if I practice personal hygiene and you don't?
Jeff:	Can I help it if you're totally selfish and I'm not? *(Makes a face)*
Samantha:	*(Makes a face back)*
Jeff:	*(Makes another face)*
Samantha:	Why, I'd like to knock that…
Jeff:	I'd like to see you try…

Have **Samantha** *and* **Jeff** *get into a brother-and-sister type fight, meaning that maybe Samantha punches him in the arm, and* **Jeff** *reacts.* **Jeff** *grabs* **Samantha's** *phone and quickly texts, "Kyle, I love you. Always have, always will" as he says it out loud for the audience to hear.* **Samantha** *recoils and comes in for the ultimate trouncing—but suddenly they both stop as though the counselor has entered the room. As they get back to their feet and* *return to their chairs,* **Jeff** *checks himself for injuries, and* **Samantha** *looks at her phone in horror.*

Samantha: Oh hi, Mr. Fleming. My name is Samantha Carmichael, and this is Jeffrey Lawrence Carmichael.

Jeff: Would you quit already? Hi, my name is Jeff Carmichael. "Lawrence" is a family name I hate. *(Shoots a stink eye at* **Samantha***)*

Samantha: Listen, Mr. Fleming. We were talking before you came in, and we just don't think there's any need for us to be here. We don't feel like these counseling sessions are necessary. So we're just going to leave now and not waste any more of your time. *(Stands up and grabs* **Jeff** *by the ear, then starts walking toward the exit)* Let's go, Jeff.

Jeff: OOOWWWW.

Samantha: *(Pauses and turns back to the counselor's chair, letting go of* **Jeff's** *ear)* What's that? *(Pause)* Of course we get along.

Jeff: No. No we don't get along. She hates me.

Samantha: *(Still trying to fool the counselor)* I don't hate him. *Hate* is such a strong word.

Jeff: No, she hates me.

Samantha: I *don't* hate him. Detest, maybe, but I don't hate him…

Jeff: She hates me, she hates me, she *(***Samantha** *grabs his ear again)* owww! Hates me!

Samantha: *(Returns to her chair)* Maybe I should explain. You see, he's always in my business. He comes in my room all the time, he…

Jeff: *(In a feminine voice)* "Kyle Jackson is such a hottie!"

Samantha: You see! I have no privacy. He just texted Kyle and confessed my undying love for him…I'm so embarrassed.

Jeff: Yes, I do everything she said! Because she and her friends are so dumb, they're funny. But yeah, I guess I shouldn't.

Samantha: You're right, you shouldn't. He does stuff like that all the time. There was this one time when I was talking on the phone...*(Stands up; **Jeff** and **Samantha** both freeze)*

Scene shifts to **Video Flashback #1** *or* **Tag Team Flashback** *across the stage.*

Note to Director: *Create a scene with your actors that would be a typical "brother-sister" type conflict. Maybe get some stories from your team and then pick the one that got the most laughs—or gasps. This way you know you've picked a very funny scene or one that would get an audience to feel bad for one of the characters. Have the actors work out the scene for either stage or film. Use the improve section in* Skit Training 101 *by The Skit Guys for more ideas about how to make this scene come alive and get finished by the time your rehearsals are over.*

Scene Two: *Back in the counselor's office.*

Samantha: You see, _____ *(Restating the scene that just occurred)* and he *(Pointing toward **Jeff**)* couldn't have cared less.

Jeff: Well, she doesn't care about any of my stuff, either. She does mean stuff to me all the time. There was this one time... *(Both Jeff and Samantha freeze again)*

Scene shifts to **Video Flashback #2** *or* **Tag Team Flashback. Samantha** *picks up the stuffed bear that's rigged so its head will come off.*

Samantha: Oh look! Little Jeffy got a stuffed bear from his little girlfriend—Mandy "Dandy" Walters.

Jeff: It's "Amanda," and give it back.

Samantha: What's the matter? Do you need your little teddy bear to take a nap?

Jeff: You're so dumb. Just give it back, or I'll...

Samantha: You'll what? You'll get upset and wet your pants? *(Grabs bear around the neck, pretending to speak for the bear)* I'm choking, Jeffy, I can't breathe, save me...

Jeff: Give it back, Samantha. *(Grabs for the bear)*

Samantha: I'm choking, I'm choking...

Jeff: *(Pulls back and tears the bear's head off)*

Samantha: Uh oh! *(They both freeze)*

Scene Three: Jeff and **Samantha** *are back in the chairs in the counselor's office.*

Jeff: That was the first gift a girl ever gave to me.

Samantha: It was just a dumb stuffed animal.

Jeff: Well, it came from a really nice store. *(To counselor)* K-Mart®.

Samantha: Okay, I guess I shouldn't have done that. *(To counselor)* What? *(Pause)* Do I love him? Oh, I get it. This is the part where we say we love each other, hug, and make up. No problem. Our parents make us do it all the time. *(To **Jeff**)* Ready? One, two, three…

Together: Sorry. *(They shallowly embrace as if they've done the "make-up hug" thing a million times)*

Samantha: *(To counselor)* How was that? *(Turns a degree more serious)* Sure, I love him. Do I like him? I didn't know I had to like him. *(She is interrupted)*

Jeff: *(Under his breath)* Yeah, I love her. Why? I don't know…I guess…

Together: *(As if they both remember at the same time)* There was this one time… *(Both freeze)*

Scene shifts to **Video Flashback #3** *or* **Tag Team Flashback. Samantha** *and* **Jeff** *sit as though* **Samantha** *is driving a car and* **Jeff** *is in the passenger seat.* **Samantha** *changes the station on the radio and likes what she hears.*

Samantha: Ooh, I like that song.

Jeff: *(Reaches out and changes the station)*

Samantha: Excuse me, I just said I like that song.

Jeff: *(In a silly mocking voice)* Excuse me, I hate that song.

Samantha: *(Turns the station back)* Excuse me, but this is my car.

Jeff: *(Changes the station again, still mocking)* Excuse me, but Mom and Dad bought this car.

Samantha:	*(Turns the station back)* If you touch that radio one more time, I am going to remove that hand from your body.
Jeff:	You're so mean.
Samantha:	*(Pleased)* I try.
Jeff:	You're the meanest girl I know.
Samantha:	I try.
Jeff:	You're the meanest boy I know.
Samantha:	*(Expression indicates that she is offended)*
Jeff:	And I was going to tell you something, but you are just too mean.
Samantha:	*(Acting as if she's not interested)* Yeah, I bet.
Jeff:	I was. I had something huge to tell you, but you're just too mean. It was HUGE.
Samantha:	*(Interested but trying to act like she's not)* Then what is it?
Jeff:	No, I can't tell you, you're too mean.
Samantha:	Just tell me.
Jeff:	If I tell you, will you promise not to make fun of me?
Samantha:	I promise.
Jeff:	Promise harder.
Samantha:	*(Indicating a strain)* I promise.
Jeff:	*(Tentative, somewhat embarrassed)* I'm going to ask out Heather Bagley.
Samantha:	*(Cannot believe her ears)* No!
Jeff:	*(In the same incredulous tone)* Yes! *(Getting down to business)* And I want you to tell me how to ask her.
Samantha:	Do you truly want to learn from my wisdom?

Jeff:	No, I want you to tell me how to ask her.
Samantha:	Just be yourself.
Jeff:	*(Disappointed)* What?
Samantha:	Just be yourself.
Jeff:	That's all you've got for me? No special tricks, no special lines. *(Mocking her tone of voice)* Just be yourself.
Samantha:	Yes, Jeff, you're great. Any girl would love to go out with you.
Jeff:	You think I'm great.
Samantha:	*(Not wanting him to get full of himself)* Yes, I think you're great.
Jeff:	And you think any girl would love to go out with me?
Samantha:	Yes.
Jeff:	*(Quickly, doing muscle flexing poses)* You're totally right; I *am* a total specimen. *(Continues to flex)*
Samantha:	Jeff?
Jeff:	Yeah.
Samantha:	Get over yourself—and get out of my car.
Jeff:	Samantha?
Samantha:	*(Slightly exasperated)* Yes, Jeff?
Jeff:	Thank you.

Scene Four *returns to* **Jeff** *and* **Samantha** *sitting in their chairs in the counselor's office. By this time they're becoming less combative and more sensitive, realizing they do love and need each other.*

Jeff:	Yeah, I guess I do need her.
Samantha:	Yeah, I guess I do need him.

Jeff: (*Looks and listens to the counselor, then turns toward **Samantha***) I'm sorry I always go into your room without asking and drive you crazy… (*Pause*) Can you forgive me?

Samantha: (*Looks and listens to the counselor, then turns toward **Jeff***) Jeff, I'm sorry I hit you a lot…

Jeff: …Yeah, you *do* hit me a lot, and it hurts…

Samantha: I'm trying to apologize here.

Jeff: Sorry.

Samantha: I'm sorry I hit you a lot, and I'm sorry I'm mean to you. (*Pause*) Can you forgive me?

Jeff: Yeah.

Jeff and **Samantha** *turn toward the counselor at the same time, then stand.*

Samantha: Well, thank you. You've been very helpful. I guess we'll see you next week. (*As if they're out of earshot of the counselor*) Hey, that wasn't so bad, was it?

Jeff: No, I guess we aren't going to kill each other after all, are we?

*At that moment, **Samantha's** phone gives a sound effect indicating she's just gotten a text. They both stop so **Samantha** can read it. We see by **Samantha's** face that it's not good.*

Jeff: Who is it?

Samantha: Kyle.

Jeff: (*Realizing it's in response to his "I love you" text*) Oh…oh…I didn't think…I mean I…what did he say?

Samantha: (*Reads text from her phone*) "I don't like you like that. Can we still be friends? Let's not make this awkward, 'kay?"

Jeff *sees that his sister is more bummed than angry.* **Jeff** *grabs her phone.*

Samantha: Jeff! What are you doing? You've already made my worst nightmares come true…

Jeff: *(Holding up a finger to say "wait a minute" as he texts, Jeff speaks out loud what he's texting)* "Sure, Kyle. Won't be awkward. This is Jeff. I did that as a joke. Sam has no idea. I will delete this as soon as I'm done. I was trying to get back at her. BTW—you are missing out on the greatest girl in the world. She's beautiful like everyone says, but her character is amazing as well. Your loss." *(Hands phone back to **Samantha**)*

Samantha *looks at* **Jeff** *and for the first time without any words, they realize they have each other's backs. They start to walk off. Then out of nowhere,* **Samantha** *hits* **Jeff** *in the arm.*

Jeff: What was that for?!

Samantha: 'Cause now I'm going to have to find someone else to have a crush on.

Jeff *hugs his sister as they exit offstage.*

Lights down.

THE END

"I'LL HAVE THE HALF-EATEN EGG ROLL, PLEASE"

**BY KNOX MCCOY, WITH REVISIONS BY TOMMY WOODARD
AND EDDIE JAMES**

WHAT: This skit represents the choices we make about the things we consume and fill our minds with as Christians.

WHO: Matt, Tyler

WHEN: Present Day

WHY: Philippians 4:8

WEAR: (COSTUMES AND PROPS) 2 large trash cans (with trash inside), a table, two chairs, an apple, a retainer, some paper plates

HOW: This skit features two casually dressed guys in a restaurant. The conversation should flow very quickly and easily.

THEMES: Old Self, Maturity, Choices, Becoming a Fully Devoted Follower of Christ

TIME: 5 minutes

The scene opens on **Matt** *and* **Tyler** *in a restaurant where orders are placed at a counter. Actors should enter from stage left, the bathroom area is stage right, and two trash cans are placed center stage.*

Tyler: *(Looking up as if examining a wall-mounted menu behind the counter)* What's good here? The menu looks great—this is going to be a tough decision.

Matt: Trust me, it's all good. I've had about everything on this menu. Love, love, love this place!

Tyler: Listen, whatever happens in here, just promise not to judge me because it's gonna get real ugly.

Matt:	Believe me, I know "ugly," and I can dance ugly circles around you when it comes to food, my friend.
Tyler:	Huh?
Matt:	Uh, nothing.
Tyler:	Hey, man, I'm going to run to the restroom real quick and wash my hands. Can't be too careful with germs and all. *(Exits stage right briefly)*
Matt:	Sounds good.

Matt *walks straight for one of the tall trash cans and begins digging various food items out of it. Disgusted patrons walk by, staring at him.*

Matt:	*(To disgusted onlookers)* What are you looking at? This is my meal…go get your own trash can.

Tyler *returns and slowly approaches* **Matt**.

Tyler:	Dude, did you lose something?
Matt:	Uh, no. Hurry up, man, there's some good stuff in here. And some creepy people over there were really eyeballing me. They may try to come claim this stuff, so hurry up and grab some grub!
Tyler:	That's funny. Now put that stuff back in the trash can before we're asked to leave.
Matt:	Can I find my lunch first? *(Pointing at second trash can)* Hey, I saw somebody throw away some chili in that trash can.
Tyler:	Seriously?
Matt:	I'm trying to find my meal here. I'M HUNGRY!
Tyler:	Stop it! I'm not joking. This is gross! *(Slides trash can away from* **Matt***)*
Matt:	DUDE?!
Tyler:	Matt, are you okay? You're digging through a public trash can for food… in a restaurant…WHERE THEY SERVE PERFECTLY GOOD FOOD. Clean food. As in "food that has not been placed in other people's mouths or touched by napkins that other people have blown their noses on."

Matt:	So what's your point?
Tyler:	Okay, wow…um…let me see if I'm getting this: You have enough money to buy yourself clean food, and you're in a restaurant that serves clean food. But you still choose to dig through the trash to find your food?
Matt:	Well, when you say it like that, it sounds weird.
Tyler:	It IS weird! It doesn't make any sense!
Matt:	Really? It makes no sense? Think about it. How much variety is in these? *(Pulls out a half-eaten apple, a retainer, and two other plates)* I've got an apple here, I've got some mashed potatoes, looks like some chewing gum, and for dessert…I think that's rock candy?
Tyler:	*(Examines plate)* I think that's a retainer.
Matt:	Guess who just saved a few thousand dollars on orthodontic work? *(Thumbs toward chest)* This guy! *(Starts to put retainer in his mouth)*
Tyler:	STOP IT!
Matt:	Look, the point is that now I'm not confined to a particular *(Does "air quotes" with fingers)* "meal plan" or *(more quotations)* "combo meal" selection. I am now master of my own cuisine, while you're just a slave to the menus provided by Corporate America.
Tyler:	*(Brief pause)* Did you practice that?
Matt:	No! *(Pause)* Okay, once or twice. *(Pause)* Okay, I practiced in the mirror, recorded it on my phone, and made some tweaks. What do you think?
Tyler:	It's good. Some real conviction there.
Matt:	Thank you.
Tyler:	But seriously…it's the TRASH. You have the option to eat delicious, nourishing, clean, rich food, but you're eating the hand-me-down, thrown-away version. That is *so* not healthy.
Matt:	Honestly? It's just so much easier for me. I mean, look at this apple *(Takes two quick bites)* Ta-da! I'm done already. I don't have to worry about, like, 12 more bites to finish it. And look at these green beans…

Tyler:	*(Gags)* Please don't. There's definitely milk mixed in with those green beans.
Matt:	*(Takes a bite)* Mmmm. Milk AND vegetables in one bite. See? It's so efficient!
Tyler:	Matt, you can tell yourself whatever you want, but you're eating trash when you don't have to. You're in one of the best restaurants in town, and you're going through the trash. I'm gonna go get some real food. *(Starts to walk toward the counter to order)*
Matt:	You're right—I don't need this garbage.
Tyler:	*(Walking off)* There ya go. Now you're making sense.
Matt:	What are you going to order, by the way?
Tyler:	*(Stops and looks at **Matt**)* Why does it matter?
Matt:	Just want to help you make the right selections, that's all…that's what friends do. *(**Tyler** starts to walk offstage again; **Matt** follows)*
Tyler:	*(In a defeated voice)* You want to eat what I throw away, don't you?
Matt:	I really do. Yes. If you could get that egg roll, I would love that. Oooh! And some of those fried won ton things! I love those! How about getting some chocolate milk…I need my protein…*(These lines are said as they both exit offstage, and by the word "protein," the lights have slowly dimmed)*

THE END

"THE LEAST OF THESE"

BY TAMI DUNCAN, WITH REVISIONS BY TOMMY WOODARD
AND EDDIE JAMES

WHAT: A game show contestant balks when she finds out the grand prize is more than she bargained for.

WHO: Hostess, Suzy, 2 Security Guards (non-speaking roles)

WHEN: Present Day

WHY: Mark 16:15; 1 Corinthians 9:24-25; Ephesians 6:7-8; Philippians 3:7

WEAR: 2 chairs, an index card, a walkie-talkie, background music
(COSTUMES
AND PROPS)

HOW: Make this set as much like a game show as you can, with the focus on **Suzy** and the **Hostess**. As for **Suzy's** character, the actress should play the role as realistically as possible because you don't want your audience to despise **Suzy**, but rather see themselves in her honest responses.

THEMES: Service, Witnessing, Missions, Selfishness, Servanthood

TIME: 5 to 7 minutes

Game Show Hostess and Suzy sit in chairs opposite each other. Hostess is holding an index card from which she'll read the final question. Background music fades in briefly.

Game Show Hostess: Welcome back to everyone's favorite game show—*The Least of These*! Our contestant Suzy here has done an amazing job so far. *(To Suzy)* Suzy, it's down to the very last question. How are you feeling?

Suzy: Like I'm going to be sick. *(Laughs nervously)*

Hostess: You're going to do just fine. Before we move on, tell us a few things about yourself.

Suzy: Oh, sure. I'd love to talk about myself. Well, I'm in my last year of college. It's been really tough this year, so I could really use a vacation! Um, right now I work a couple of days a week with the youth at a church, helping them know more about God, which is fun but tiring; two days a week is plenty! And I'm dating a great guy who's watching right now. *(Turns to the "camera" and waves)* Hi, Scott!

Hostess: Wonderful! Now, just out of curiosity, have you ever seen our game show?

Suzy: No, I've never watched this show, *but* I've heard you give away amazing trips that are like no other. I'm excited about that!

Hostess: Okay, well let's move on to your very last question. If you answer this correctly, you'll walk away with the grand prize. And every person in this audience wants you to win this prize—you've played a fabulous game! *(Very seriously)* But if you answer this question wrong...you'll walk away with nothing. Are you ready for your final question?

Suzy: *(Nervously excited)* Yes! I am *so* ready!

Hostess: Here's the question: *(Music plays in the background; she reads from her note card)* Name the second greatest commandment according to Christ.

Suzy: *(Thinking)* Okay, I should know this. Um...command, commandment, commander. Come on, Suzy...you know this.

Hostess: *(Interrupts)* You have three seconds.

Suzy: I think I'm going with *(Cringes)*...Love your neighbor.

Hostess: Is that your answer?

Suzy: *(Pause, closes eyes)* Yes! That's my answer. *(Crosses fingers)* Love your neighbor as yourself.

Hostess: Suzy...*(Pause)* you've won the grand prize!

Suzy *is ecstatic; she jumps out of her chair, and the expression on her face is one of amazement—she can't believe she won. She's fanning away tears, repeating things like, "Oh my goodness, oh my goodness! I can't believe it. This is impossible. I've never won anything!"*

Hostess:	Suzy, do you want to know what you've won?
Suzy:	I don't know if I can handle it...but...YES!
Hostess:	You've won a whole week...
Suzy:	*(Still fanning her face, she returns to her chair looking like she's about to faint)* Oh my goodness...
Hostess:	...in a village *(Pause)* in India, where there's no running water or electricity or beds. There you'll have the *privilege* of working alongside the village women, gathering food and water, serving meals, and *(Chuckles)* swatting at flies, no doubt.
Suzy:	*(Horrified; stumbling through her words)* What? But...I...I thought I... you know...would get...is this a joke?
Hostess:	No! This is a chance of a *lifetime* to go and serve people who really, really need it. I can't imagine the beautiful smiles on those faces when they see that *you*, Suzy, have come to serve them.
Suzy:	But that's not what I...um...that's not what I...
Hostess:	*(Concerned)* That's not what you...*what?*
Suzy:	That's not what I *wanted. (Starts to cry through her words)* I *wanted* a beautiful sandy beach with crystal clear water and a resort to stay in with an amazing bed and big fluffy pillows and a huge soaker tub where I could put in lots of bubbles. And of course the food would be all-you-can-eat, and it would taste amazing, and Nick Jonas would be there to give me a surprise serenade... *(A little embarrassed at her rambling)* That's what I thought I *might* be getting. The other trip sounds kind of... dirty and not very relaxing, you know?
Hostess:	Oh, well, so you don't like your prize?
Suzy:	No, I don't. And I don't want to go on a trip like that. That's asking too much of me. That's not even a prize—no running water? No electricity? Are you kidding? I wouldn't survive a week! I want to relax and have fun. You tricked me...the grand prize was supposed to be about *me.*
Hostess:	Suzy, *(Leans forward and kind of talks under her breath so as to not embarrass **Suzy** in front of the audience)* you're a Christian, right?

Suzy:	*(Yells)* YES! (**Hostess**, *startled, jumps back in her seat*) I'm a Christian, but all of that kind of stuff is for missionaries and pastors, not *me*. This was supposed to be a vacation for *me*; a getaway with nothing to do but lie on the beach.
Hostess:	But this is one of those *amazing* trips you've heard about. Don't you realize that when you go and serve those people, Jesus says you're actually serving him? We're giving you an all-expenses-paid trip to serve Christ like you've never served him before. And in the process, you'll be helping change and save people's lives!
Suzy:	*(Tears are turning to anger)* I can't even imagine how that could be true. *(Gets serious and up in the **Hostess's** face)* Look, lady, I came here to win a prize—a *big* prize—and if I don't get it…
Hostess:	*(Pulls a walkie-talkie out of her pocket and calmly says…)* Security.

The 2 **Security Guards** *come out to escort* **Suzy** *off the stage.*

Suzy:	I have two *huge* dogs that can slash your tires with their teeth! *(The guys pick her up as she squirms and kicks her legs; they all exit as she yells)* I want the smell of tanning lotion!
Hostess:	*(To audience)* Well, that concludes our show where *our* game is played by different rules—the prize will come, but it comes as a result of first giving of yourselves and becoming servants to this hurting world. It's a prize that can last a lifetime. Thanks for watching our show! *(She exits to the same music played earlier)*

THE END

"THE NARROW WAY"

BY GINNYLEE ELLIS, WITH REVISIONS BY TOMMY WOODARD AND EDDIE JAMES

SKIT
5.5

WHAT: An airline passenger makes a strange request that defies reality, highlighting that there really is only one way to make it through life successfully.

WHO: Passenger (male), Attendant (female), Pilot (offstage)

WHEN: Present Day

WHY: Matthew 7:13-14; Luke 13:22-30; John 14:6

WEAR: 2 chairs resembling airplane seats (if possible), small bags of peanuts, a sheet
(COSTUMES of paper
AND PROPS)

HOW: This skit raises a very good point for people who are hoping to find other ways to God besides Jesus Christ. You also have the opportunity to give non-speaking parts to less experienced students to make the scene look as realistic as possible (other passengers, second flight attendant, etc.).

THEMES: Excuses, Salvation, Selfishness, Compromise

TIME: 7 minutes

The scene opens on a commercial airline flight. A **Passenger** *takes his seat as the* **Pilot** *speaks over the intercom.*

Pilot: *(Offstage)* Good morning again, ladies and gentlemen! We're now at our cruising altitude of 37,000 feet. We're flying with a slight tailwind today, so we'll have no problem getting to Denver on time. In fact, we may be a few minutes early. Just sit back and enjoy the rest of our flight, and thank you for flying TransAmerica Airlines.

Passenger: *(As* **Attendant** *walks by)* Miss? Oh, Miss?

Attendant: Yes, how can I help you?

Passenger: I have an unusual request, and I hope you don't consider me presumptuous for asking.

Attendant: TransAmerica Airlines is here to make sure you have the best possible travel experience. We want to do everything we can to serve you. Please don't feel embarrassed to ask for a favor. Do you need a blanket or pillow?

Passenger: Oh no, it's nothing like that. I have several business appointments in downtown Denver, and I need to get there as expeditiously as possible.

Attendant: Well, when we get to Denver, several of our customer service staff will be there to help passengers find the gates to their connecting flights. If you ask one of them, they can direct you to ground transportation. You could catch a taxi downtown or ride one of the shuttles. You should be able to find something convenient and quick.

Passenger: Well, that's not exactly what I had in mind. The airport is a long way from downtown, and I was hoping we could actually land somewhere closer to the downtown area.

Passenger *opens a tiny bag of peanuts and begins eating them one peanut at a time. Have fun with this part.*

Attendant: *(Long pause as Attendant tries to process this insane request)* I don't think I understand. This flight lands at Denver International. I'm not aware of a downtown airport in Denver.

Passenger: I know. I guess my request is this: Is there any way the pilot could land the plane on *(Looks at a piece of paper)* 2nd Street in downtown Denver?

Attendant: Excuse me?

Passenger: Yes, well, you see, it would really simplify everything for me. I could just hop off, and one of your people could find my bags and toss them out. Then I'd be there in plenty of time to make my appointments and get checked into the hotel early. I'd so hoped to do a little shopping before dinner tonight. *(Continues to eat peanuts)*

Attendant: *(Another very long pause for humor as* **Attendant** *processes just how insane this guy is)* I don't mean to be rude, but you can't be serious. If we even think about landing anywhere except our assigned runway, our flight crew would get into a tremendous amount of trouble. And besides that, changing our flight plan would put us, the rest of the passengers, and a lot of innocent people on 2nd Street in very serious danger.

Passenger: Yes, well, I'm sure there would be a few details to work out, but you people are professionals. You get paid to work out these little problems. By the way, can I get some more of these yummy peanuts?

Attendant: *(Stares at him for a moment then reaches into her pocket and grabs another bag of peanuts for him)* Sir, this is NOT a little problem. Granting your request would jeopardize hundreds of lives. Try to understand this: There is one way—and only one way—to reach our destination safely. We have to land squarely in the middle of our assigned runway. In fact, we'd be in danger if only ONE wheel got anywhere CLOSE to the edge of that runway.

Passenger: Well, that's a bit narrow-minded, isn't it? It's a big world, and surely there are lots of places and lots of ways to land this plane.

Attendant: Yes, but there's only ONE place and ONE way for this plane to land SAFELY. We have to land in the middle of that runway!

Passenger: Well, there's no need to get huffy about it.

Attendant: *(Restraining anger)* You're exactly right. I'm sorry. Now, is there any other way I can help you?

Passenger: Um…well, in that case, I guess I could use a pillow and a blanket.

Attendant: I'm sorry—we're all out. Have a nice flight!

Passenger: Well, I never! *(Looks around)* I'll just have to speak to another attendant. *(Signals another attendant farther up the aisle)* Hello! I have an unusual request, and I hope you don't consider me presumptuous for asking…

Lights down.

THE END

ENSEMBLES

"THE LOST SHEEP"
BY BRIAN CROPP, WITH REVISIONS BY TOMMY WOODARD AND EDDIE JAMES

WHAT: This skit is a light parable of how often we choose rebellion even when we know that obedience is best for us.

WHO: Narrator, Shepherd, Biff the Lost Sheep, Hobo, Salesperson, Girl, Other Sheep (plural)

WHEN: Present Day

WHY: Luke 15:3-7, 11-32

WEAR: (COSTUMES AND PROPS) Fake money, a wallet, "raggedy clothes" for the Hobo, white pants and shirts for the Sheep, black pants and shirt for Biff, a business suit for the Salesperson

HOW: This skit should be done as an imitation or parody of a children's show, somewhere along the lines of *Yo Gabba Gabba!* or *Barney*. The campier the skit, the better it will play and help soften some of its harsher themes.

THEMES: Rebellion, Obedience, Grace, Trust, Forgiveness

TIME: 4 minutes

The **Narrator** *addresses the audience. A herd of* **Sheep** *and the* **Shepherd** *are center stage.*

Narrator: Once upon a time, on a grassy hill, there lived a Shepherd...

Shepherd: *(To audience)* Hiya.

Narrator: ...and his sheep.

Sheep: Baaaaaaa.

Narrator: All of the sheep loved the Shepherd.

Biff: Ahem!

Narrator:	They loved the times he would…
Biff:	AHEM!
Narrator:	Pardon?
Biff:	*(Threateningly)* Not everyone.
Narrator:	My mistake. Not everyone. Well, there's always one lost sheep in the family. *(Pointing to Biff)* This is Biff.
Biff:	*(To audience)* I gotta get outta this place. I mean, look at it! "The Man" has got us locked in this pen. We only get to leave when *he* lets us out. We only get to eat when *he* tells us to. I mean, look at these followers! They'd do anything he wants them to do. *(Pause)* Well, as soon as the sun goes down tonight, I'm breakin' out of here. You don't believe me? Just you watch.
Narrator:	*(Biff acts out his plan as the Narrator speaks)* Sure enough, when the sun went down and the Shepherd went to sleep, Biff took $300 from the Shepherd's wallet and made his getaway.

Hobo *enters.*

Biff:	I know what you're thinkin'…that at the end of this story I go back to the Shepherd and everything turns out "peachy keen." Well, it's not gonna happen, get me? 'Cause now I'm free, and I'm never going back.
Hobo:	Pssst!
Biff:	I'm off to make my fortune!
Hobo:	Pssst! Buddy.
Biff:	Huh?
Hobo:	Spare a dollar for a poor man?
Biff:	Get away from me. I've got no time for you.

Hobo *exits.* **Salesperson** *enters.*

Narrator:	And the Lost Sheep went on his way. He met a salesperson.

Biff:	Who are you?
Salesperson:	Pay attention. I'm a salesperson.
Biff:	Really? You make good money?
Salesperson:	Yep.
Biff:	You set your own hours?
Salesperson:	Oh yeah.
Biff:	Got nobody telling you what to do?
Salesperson:	Let me tell you: When you're out on the road, there ain't nothing, nobody, nowhere gonna tell you what to do. You are your own…well…sheep.
Biff:	This could be my lucky break!
Salesperson:	Well, first you need to get the "How to Sell" start-up kit.
Biff:	Start-up kit. *(Waits for more information)* Uh huh.
Salesperson:	Well?
Biff:	Well what?
Salesperson:	Well, the start-up kit costs two-fifty.
Biff:	Two hundred and fifty dollars?
Salesperson:	Yes. Now, it's a sizable investment—but isn't your freedom worth that much?
Biff:	You're right. I've got to stop playing it safe and live! *(Shells out the money)*
Salesperson:	Wise decision. Wise decision. You should receive that kit in the next coupla days. *(Exits)*
Narrator:	Later on, realizing he'd been scammed, Biff goes to hunt down the salesperson.

Girl *enters.*

Biff: That's right, I'm gonna hunt that cheater down!

Girl: Hello.

Biff: And I'm gonna grind his bones into a…

Girl: *(Getting his attention)* Hello?

Biff: Hello.

Girl: I was wondering…

Biff: Yes?

Girl: Well, here I am all alone, and there you are…and well, I was wondering if you'd buy me dinner.

Biff: Uh, sure. What are you in the mood for?

Girl: How much money you got?

Biff: *(Holding out money)* Fifty dollars.

Girl: It'll probably cost that much. *(Grabs money and runs offstage)* I just love lamb chops!

Biff: Hey, wait! You're not supposed to do that!

Biff *tries to chase the* **Girl***, but he trips and falls. He lays there, defeated.*

Narrator: Meanwhile, the Shepherd noticed that one of his sheep was lost. So he went out to look for him. And when the Shepherd found the lost sheep wandering aimlessly, he picked him up and took him home.

As the **Narrator** *reads that last part, the* **Shepherd** *should come onstage and pantomime as if he's calling out for* **Biff** *while* **Biff** *walks around aimlessly. Once they meet up,* **Biff** *should look at the* **Shepherd** *as if he's going to get in trouble. However, the* **Shepherd** *should smile and pick up* **Biff** *as if he were holding a baby. You'll need to work on this part ahead of time to make it as smooth as possible.*

Biff: How'd you find me?

Shepherd: You think I don't know you or how attracted you are to the things just outside my pen? I knew just where to find you.

Biff: But then you must know that I don't want to be here. There are too many rules. There's no freedom for me to express myself.

Shepherd: Don't you understand yet? There's more freedom *inside* my protection than outside of it. But I understand you. Just remember that you can run away your whole life—but I will always know where to find you.

Narrator: And while the Lost Sheep recovered from his wounds, the Shepherd still watched his flock—just as he'd always done.

Biff: *(Pointing offstage)* I wonder what's over there?

Narrator: The end.

Lights down.

THE END

"HEAD VS. HEART"

BY REBECCA WIMMER

WHAT: This skit portrays a game show that pits one contestant with great biblical head knowledge against a fellow Christian whose relationship with Jesus comes from the heart.

WHO: Host, Christian 1, Christian 2, Extras (optional)

WHEN: Present Day

WHY: Proverbs 11:2; Matthew 11:29; 2 Corinthians 5:12

WEAR:
(COSTUMES AND PROPS)
Christian 1 and Christian 2 should wear casual clothes. The Host can wear a cheesy polyester suit and even a bad toupee. Also needed are index cards for the Host to hold, 2 podiums or stands (one for each contestant), 2 desk bells or "Ding!" sound effects when contestants ring in, APPLAUSE signs, and a "boing" or buzzer sound effect for wrong answers.

HOW: Keep things moving and at a good pace. The Host should have lots of energy. Christian 1 is very smug and confident in his or her head knowledge, while Christian 2 is a new believer with a much humbler attitude. Be sure to work with your sound person so all the buzzer/boing sound effects happen on cue. The Extras may be used to hold up an APPLAUSE sign or keep score.

THEMES: Wisdom, Knowledge, Relationship, Being Real

TIME: 7 to 9 minutes

---

*The **Host** enters.*

Host: Welcome to *Head vs. Heart*, the trivia game show that pits mind against moral matter! I'm your host, Jerry Junderbink! Today is our special teen edition of the show, so please join me in welcoming our dueling Christians! *(**Extras** hold up* APPLAUSE *signs as **Christian 1** and **Christian 2** enter to take their places behind their podiums with a bell or signal in front of each of them.)* Christian 1 and Christian 2, tell us a little bit about yourselves!

Christian 1:   Well, I've been a *(Makes "air quotes" with fingers)* "Christian" all my life. I've attended Sunday school since I was knee-high to a grasshopper, I'm on my church's Bible trivia team, and I own 17 Bibles.

Host: That's amazing! Christian 2, it's your turn.

Christian 2:   Uh, well…I'm a new Christian. I just accepted Jesus on the last youth retreat we went on. So this is kind of new to me still. I haven't gone to church since I was little. I just started coming again about a year ago. I own a Bible now—my youth director got me one the second time I showed up to youth group. I've also started going to a small group. So yeah…that's been cool.

Host: Excellent! All right, Christians—hands on your signaling devices because we're ready to start! Christian 1, you won the coin toss backstage, so you choose first.

Christian 1:   I'll take Old Testament Prophets for 200, Job.

Host: He appeared with Moses during the transfiguration of Jesus, and before that he was taken up to heaven in a fiery chariot.

Christian 1 *hits his button making a "DING!"*

Christian 1:   Elijah!

Host: That's correct, for 200 points. Choose again.

Christian 1:   Let's jump to the Book of Revelation for 600.

Boing/Buzzer noise

Host: Oh, I'm sorry! That noise means you've just been trampled by the Four Horsemen of the Apocalypse! You lose your turn. Christian 2, the board is yours!

Christian 2:   Okay, I'll take the Life of Jesus for 100.

Host: How old was Jesus when he was crucified on the cross?

Christian 2:   Uh…umm…

Buzzer noise

Host: I'm sorry—time is up! Christian 1, you can steal!

Christian 1: So easy! Jesus was approximately 33 years old when he died.

Host: That is correct! 100 points go to Christian 1!

Christian 1: *(To Christian 2)* How could you miss that one?

Host: Christian 1, you have the choice of the board.

Christian 1: I'll take Christianity in Real Life for 300, Job.

Host: True or False: Copying another person's homework is cheating.

Christian 1: *(Presses button for "Ding!")* Well, it's not like you're copying test answers, and I do it all the time…so, false!

Host: Ooooh…I'm sorry. That is incorrect! Christian 2, it's yours to steal!

Christian 2: Well, they're not *your* answers, so…yeah, it's cheating. I'll say true!

Host: That's correct! 300 points for Christian 2. You're on the board, and the choice is yours.

Christian 2: I'll take—

Loud siren noise

Host: That noise means it's Rapid-Fire Trivia time! Christians, place your hands on your signals. Each of these questions is worth 100 points. Ready? Let's go! The Bible records this man as the oldest person ever!

Christian 1: *(Ding!)* Methuselah! *(pronounced "meh-thoo-sell-ahh")*

Host: Correct! He was swallowed by a giant fish!

Christian 1: *(Ding!)* Jonah!

Host: That's right! She became Queen of Persia after Xerxes dethroned his previous queen!

Christian 1: *(Ding!)* Esther!

Host: Right again! What is the fifth of the Ten Commandments?

Christian 1:	*(Ding!)* Duh! Honor your mother and father!
Host:	Correct! This man's donkey knew how to talk!
Christian 1:	*(Ding!)* Balaam!
Host:	You're on fire! How many chapters make up the book of Psalms?
Christian 1:	*(Ding!)* One hundred and fifty!
Host:	He killed his brother Abel and became the first murderer on earth!
Christian 1:	*(Ding!)* Cain! Give me something harder!
Host:	He was anointed the very first king of Israel.
Christian 1:	*(Ding!)* Saul! Next!
Host:	He built an ark and put... ′
Christian 1:	*(Ding!)* Too easy! Noah!
Host:	Name the 12 sons of Jacob.
Christian 1:	*(Ding!)* Reuben, Simeon, Levi, Naphtali, Isaachar, Asher, Dan, Zebulun, Gad, Judah, Joseph, and Benjamin!
Host:	That is correct and that ends the round! *(**Extras** hold up* APPLAUSE *signs)* Congratulations, Christian 1, you swept that round and earned 1,000 points! That puts your total at 1,300 points so far. Christian 2, you have 300 points, and as the contender with the lowest total, you may choose first this round.
Christian 2:	Uh, okay. Let's go with, um...Kings and Queens of the Bible for 200.
Host:	She was the wife of King Ahab, renowned for her wickedness.
Christian 1:	*(Ding!)* Queen Jezebel!
Host:	Yes! One hundred bonus points if you can tell us how she died.
Christian 1:	She was thrown out of a window and eaten by dogs.
Host:	That is correct!

Christian 2:	What?! That's in the Bible?
Host:	Interesting, isn't it?
Christian 2:	"Weird" is what it is.

Buzzer noise, **Extras** *hold up* APPLAUSE *signs*

Host:	And that sound marks the end of the round. So our Christian with the lowest score gets to choose the final Rapid-Fire category.
Christian 2:	All right, then, let's go back to Christianity in Real Life.
Host:	All right, Christians. Each question in this Rapid-Fire category is worth 200 points. Hands on your signals. And here we go! When your mom ticks you off by grounding you for talking back to her, what should you do?
Christian 1:	*(Ding!)* Scream, "I hate you," stomp your feet all the way to your room, and slam the door!
Host:	Incorrect!
Christian 2:	*(Ding!)* Apologize for talking back and accept your parent's discipline.
Host:	Correct for 200 points! What does the Bible teach about how we're supposed to treat our enemies?
Christian 1:	*(Ding!)* Well, it says to love them, but it doesn't really mean that.
Host:	No, I'm sorry, that's wrong. Christian 2?
Christian 2:	Jesus says to love our enemies…so we should love our enemies.
Host:	Correct! Next question: A weird kid at your school drops his books all over the floor in the hallway. What do you do?
Christian 1:	*(Ding!)* You point and laugh really hard and keep on walking!
Host:	No!
Christian 2:	*(Ding!)* You help him pick up his stuff?
Host:	Correct again! You're invited to an unsupervised party where you know alcohol will be present—what do you do?

Christian 1:	*(Ding!)* Party! Jesus is for Sundays.
Host:	Wrong.
Christian 2:	*(Ding!)* You don't go.
Host:	Correct for 200 more points! Your little brother wants to borrow something of yours. What do you say?
Christian 1:	*(Ding!)* Oh, heck no!
Christian 2:	*(Ding!)* Of course! Just please respect my property.
Host:	That's right! Your significant other asks you to "go further" than you think God wants you to go in your relationship. What do you do?
Christian 1:	*(Ding!)* You say…
Host:	*(Cutting **Christian 1** off abruptly, already anticipating an incorrect answer)* WRONG! Christian 2?
Christian 2:	Just say no and then reevaluate this relationship as to whether or not it's helping or hindering your walk with God.
Host:	CORRECT AGAIN! You and your friends are at the mall. They encourage you to steal a shirt you can't afford. You…?
Christian 2:	*(Ding!)* No!
Host:	Correct! Your friends are throwing rocks at cars, and you…?
Christian 2:	*(Ding!)* No!
Host:	Correct! Your friends are pressuring you to—
Christian 2:	*(Ding!)* No!
Host:	Correct again! Following Jesus means that you—
Christian 1:	*(Ding!)* Go to church on Sundays and…yeah, that's pretty much it.
Host:	Christian 2?
Christian 2:	Um, love God by loving others every day and in everything you do?

Host: That is…CORRECT! We've reached the end of the game, and Christian 2—you've pulled ahead! Congratulations—you win!

Extras *hold up* APPLAUSE *signs.*

Christian 1: What?! But Christian 2 didn't know who Noah was, or about the prophets, or even the tribes of Israel! None of that! How can he/she win?

Host: No, Christian 2 may not have all of your head knowledge, and he/she's working on that. But his/her heart knowledge has made him/her a champion.

Extras *hold up* APPLAUSE *signs. The* **Host** *shakes* **Christian 2's** *hand while he/she smiles and waves at the audience.* **Christian 1** *pouts and stomps offstage.*

Lights down.

THE END

SKIT 5.8

"OH MY WORD"
BY BEN GAZAWAY

WHAT: Through a series of entangled phone conversations, four teenagers create more questions than answers.

WHO: Melissa, Carissa, Alyssa, David (4 teenagers)

WHEN: Present Day

WHY: Proverbs 11:3; 16:28; 2 Corinthians 12:20

WEAR: (COSTUMES AND PROPS) Each actor needs a cell phone, and all are dressed as typical teenagers. Actors can be seated or standing. NOTE: If you have a good sound person, prepare "ringtones" ahead of time for each person, instead of having the actors make the ringing noise.

HOW: The actors should be encouraged to ham it up with lots of energy and fast pacing to make the play on their names even more effective and funny.

THEMES: Gossip, Lying, Truth, Honesty

TIME: 3 to 5 minutes

---

*The lights come up on two girls, **Melissa** and **Carissa**, who are standing on opposite sides of the stage while facing the audience.*

Melissa: *(Calling on her cell phone)* Brrrrring, brrrring… *(Or recorded ringtone)*

Carissa: *(Answering her phone)* Uhh, hello?

Melissa: Carissa?

Carissa: Oh hey, Melissa!

Melissa: Hey girl, whatchu doin'?

Carissa: Not much, just watching *Camp Rock 9*…can you believe the Jonas

	Brothers are still rock stars?
Melissa:	Totally! But that girl looks like a chinchilla.
Carissa:	*(Laughs obnoxiously and snorts)* Oh…my…word! Girl, you are LOL funny!
Melissa:	Hey, speaking of chinchilla, did you see what Alyssa was wearing today?
Carissa:	Oh…my…word! Can you believe she'd wear a…hang on; I've got a call coming in. *(Clicking over)* Uhh, hello?
Alyssa:	Hey, Carissa.
Carissa:	Oh hey, Alyssa! Whatchu doin'?
Alyssa:	Not much, just watching *Twilight 6*.
Carissa:	Oh…my…word. I LOVE that movie!
Alyssa:	Oh…MY…word—I've got a serious crush on that dude who turns into a chinchilla.
Carissa:	TMI, girl. But hey, speaking of chinchillas, did you hear what David said to Melissa today?
Alyssa:	Oh…my…word! Like, I can't believe he called her a…hang on; I've got another call. *(Clicking over)* Uhh, hello?
David:	Hello, Alyssa?
Alyssa:	*(In a flirty voice)* Hey David, whatchu doin'?
David:	Nothing. Just watching *When Chinchillas Attack*…it's part of Chinchilla Week on the Discovery Channel.
Alyssa:	Oh…my…word! I saw you changed your relationship status to "I'm not really sure, you'll have to ask my stupid girlfriend"…so are you and Melissa broken up?
David:	Uhh, I guess so. Hey, what are you doing on Friday…hang on; I've got a call coming in. *(Clicking over)* Uhh, hello?
Melissa:	So are you not talking to me anymore?

David:	We talked like 10 minutes ago!
Melissa:	Yeah, well, I saw your relationship status on Facebook, and we need to DTR.
David:	DTR? I thought we were broken up!
Melissa:	How can I be your "stupid girlfriend" if we're broken up?
David:	Good point. Can you hang on a second? *(Tries to click over to previous call)* Hey Alyssa, I can't do Friday night—apparently Melissa and I are still going out.
Melissa:	It's still me, you doofus! Oh...my...word! You were going to go out with Alyssa?! Hang on a second. *(Clicks over)* Carissa! David just asked out Alyssa!
Carissa:	Oh...my...word! Girl, hang on. *(Clicks over)* Hey, Alyssa, why did you ask out David when you knew he was going out with Melissa?
Alyssa:	Oh...my...word! Girl, I didn't ask him out, he was about to ask ME out! Hang on a second. *(Clicks over)* David, why did you tell Melissa that I asked you out?
David:	Is that what she said? *(Upset)* That's it! Hang on a second. *(Clicks over)* I want to break up!
Alyssa:	But we haven't even gone out on a date!
David:	*(Clicks over again)* I just want you to know that we're finally broken up.
Melissa:	Broken up? I thought we just got back together?! You're such a jerk! *(Clicks over)* Oh...my...word, David is SUCH a jerk!
David:	It's still me.
Melissa:	*(Clicks over)* Oh...my...word! David is SUCH a jerk!
Carissa:	I told you he was a jerk. Hang on—I'm calling him now.
David:	*(Clicks over)* Hello?
Carissa:	David, I just wanted to say that you're a jerk and everyone thinks you look like a wanna-be Jonas Brother vampire chinchilla!

David:	*(Clicks over)* I can't believe you said I look like a wanna-be Jonas Brother vampire chinchilla!
Alyssa:	I didn't say that! Melissa must have said that! Put her on conference!
David:	Hang on. *(Clicks over)* Melissa, I can't believe you said I look like a wanna-be Jonas Brother vampire chinchilla!
Melissa:	I never said that! Carissa must have said that! Put her on conference!
David:	*(Clicks over)* Why did YOU call me a *(Pause)* chinchilla?
Carissa:	I didn't!

All the girls start arguing among themselves about who called whom a chinchilla.

| David: | *(Reaching his limit)* That's it! I'm breaking up with all of you! |
| All the Girls: | Fine! |

They all slam their cell phones shut or forcefully hang up.

Melissa:	*(Making another call on her phone)* Brrrring…brrrring *(Or recorded ringtone)*
Carissa:	Uhh, hello?
Melissa:	Hey girl, whatchu doin'?

Lights down.

THE END

SKIT 5.9

"OUTSIDE THE MOB"
BY REBECCA WIMMER

WHAT: A high school girl decides she can no longer sit idly by while an innocent person is bullied by others.

WHO: 3 Mean Girls (Shannon, Alexandria, and Kim), Lacie, Kaylee

WHEN: Present Day

WHY: Psalm 82:3; Proverbs 31:9; Ephesians 4:32

WEAR:
(COSTUMES AND PROPS) Shannon, Alexandria, Kim, and Kaylee are dressed as typical high school girls. One or more of them could be dressed as a cheerleader or wearing a letter jacket. Lacie, however, should be dressed in a drastically different style, perhaps "alternative" and mostly in black. The setting is a school lunchroom with two tables and some chairs. Lacie has a portfolio of her drawings sitting next to her. Kaylee has a Bible.

HOW: Be very careful with this one. It will be easy to make this cheesy or overly dramatic. So play it as realistically as possible. Kaylee should talk to the audience as if they're her conscience. Let the mean girls' words do the work; they don't need to get physical.

THEMES: Cruelty, Bullying, Love, Defending Others

TIME: 5 minutes

---

*As the scene opens, there are two tables on opposite sides of the stage. On stage right sits **Lacie** with her portfolio of drawings and her lunch. She is by herself. On stage left is another table where **Kaylee** sits, also eating her lunch and reading her Bible.*

Shannon, Alexandria, and Kim *walk in stage right. They march over to where **Lacie** is sitting and surround her.*

Shannon: Well, lookie here...it's Lacie Shoop. Lacie, do you know what rhymes with *Shoop*?

Lacie: (*Obviously wants to be somewhere else, but she is shy and afraid of the girls*) Soup?

Shannon: Lacie, do you know what other words rhyme with *Shoop*?

Lacie: (*Meekly*) Yes, I know what else rhymes with *Shoop*.

The scene freezes as **Kaylee** *stands up with her Bible in her arms.*

Kaylee: (*To audience*) That's Lacie Shoop. She just moved here from California. Every day at lunch she sits by herself, and every day at lunch she gets picked on by these three girls.

The scene resumes.

Alexandria: Lacie, we all saw you looking at Jeff in the hallway today.

Lacie: (*Trying to explain herself*) He dropped a book, and I just picked it up for him.

Kim: Lacie, if my boyfriend needs something, I'LL be the one who takes care of it, understand?

Shannon: You'd have your own boyfriend if you were just a little prettier…

The scene freezes.

Kaylee: (*To audience*) I've been watching this go on for weeks, and every day I come to lunch saying I'm going to do something about it. And every day I end up just watching it all unfold in front of me.

The scene resumes.

Alexandria: (*Picking up* **Lacie's** *portfolio and feigning interest*) So, Lacie, what's a loser like you doing tonight for homecoming?

Kim: Besides stalking other people's boyfriends.

Shannon: There's probably a Harry Potter marathon on TV for someone like you, huh?

The scene freezes.

Kaylee: (*To audience*) You know the safest place is in the middle of the mob... you know, safety in numbers? I mean, even if I say something to them, they'll just start bullying me too, right? Besides, it's the teachers' job to stop bullying.

The scene resumes.

Kim: So Mr. Hammond told us he's been watching us...he said he heard someone was getting bullied around here.

Shannon: We told him he needs to be watching you, Lacie POOP, because you were making threats on Facebook.

Lacie: That's not true!

Alexandria: (*Leaning in and hissing*) Listen, I've been offered scholarships from three Division 1 schools, so if you think I'm gonna let you ruin that with your big mouth, then you're crazy.

The scene freezes.

Kaylee: (*To audience*) You know, Jesus never wavered when it came to sticking up for what was right. Whether it was stopping the crowd from stoning a woman or hanging out with tax collectors and "sinners," Jesus often found himself on the wrong side of a mob. The outside.

The scene resumes.

Shannon: Lacie, you better be careful. You're going to get hurt one of these days.

The scene freezes.

Kaylee: It's too bad Jesus isn't here to defend Lacie Shoop...or is he?

The scene resumes.

Kim: Yeah, you better keep your big freakish mouth shut if you know what's good for you.

Kaylee *walks over and sits down next to* **Lacie.**

Kaylee: (*To* **Lacie**) Hey, do you mind if I sit here?

Lacie: *(A bit confused and somewhat relieved)* Uh…no. You can sit there.

Shannon, Kim, and Alexandria *watch* **Kaylee** *sit down, and they can't believe what they see.*

Kaylee: Hey ladies, how are things going with the homecoming preparations?

Shannon: I can't believe you're actually sitting with that loser!

Kim: Have fun in Loserville.

The three girls exit stage left.

Kaylee: *(To **Lacie**)* Hi, I'm Kaylee.

Lacie: I'm Lacie.

Kaylee: It's good to finally meet you.

Lights down.

THE END

SKIT 5.10

"THE HUDDLE"
BY GINNYLEE ELLIS, WITH REVISIONS BY TOMMY WOODARD AND EDDIE JAMES

WHAT: A football huddle is a safe, feel-good time for a few football players, but will they ever decide to actually play the game?

WHO: Player 1, Player 2, Player 3, Player 4, Player 5, Referee

WHEN: Present Day

WHY: Matthew 28:18-20; Acts 1:8

WEAR: (COSTUMES AND PROPS) Football and referee uniforms are needed, as well as a whistle for the ref. But it should be noted that the Players should hold their helmets, rather than wear them, so as not to restrict the view of their facial expressions.

HOW: There is a risk that this skit will feel very static if you're not careful. It will rely a lot on the facial expressions of the four players in the huddle, as well as the two characters outside of it. Also keep in mind that the football characters should be played as tough guys, even when they share their feelings.

THEMES: Complacency, Action in Life, Football, 5th Quarter, Power, Fear

TIME: 5 to 7 minutes

Players 1–4 *are in a huddle in the center of the stage.*

Player 1: We've got a great huddle here! I really want to thank you guys for being a part of it.

Player 2: I appreciate just being invited. I'd been looking for a good huddle, and I'm thankful that I finally found one.

Player 3: I feel the same way. We've really gotten close since we formed this huddle, and I just want you to know that you guys are very important to me.

Player 1: You're very important to us, too. Thanks for saying that!

Player 3:   Don't mention it! We're just glad to have you—glad to have all of you.

Player 4:   Yeah, I've been all over the world, and this huddle is the best thing I've ever been a part of. I just hope we can keep it together.

Referee blows the whistle.

Referee: (To audience) We have a delay of game on the offense. That's a five-yard penalty. It's still first down. (To **Players 1–4**) That's the third straight delay of game penalty! Are you guys ever going to run a play?

Player 1:   Thanks for your interest, Mr. Ref. We'll get around to running a play soon. Right now, we're building our relationship here in this huddle.

Referee: Well, you're gonna "build" your way right into your own end zone. Now, hurry up and do something.

Player 5:   (Enters as if from the bench) What are you guys doing? Coach is going nuts!

Player 4:   Are we going to let HIM be a part of the huddle?

Player 1:   He is wearing the same jersey.

Player 4:   Yeah, but I don't know him that well.

Player 1:   Let's just hear what he has to say, and then we'll make up our minds.

Player 5:   Coach said to run 65-toss power trap. Now let's go!

Player 4:   I THOUGHT he was going to be trouble.

Player 1:   I guess you were right. Well, we don't have to listen to what he says.

Player 2:   Aw, gee, I don't really like 65-toss power trap. It's too hard.

Player 3:   Yeah, I'm just supposed to block on that play. I never get to carry the ball.

Player 5:   Hank, you're a tackle. You're SUPPOSED to block.

Player 3:   Well, I could carry the ball once in a while. The other team wouldn't expect that.

Player 5:   They wouldn't expect it because you're slow as Christmas! J. J. runs the ball—he's the running back.

Player 2:	It seems to me that Hank has some issues we need to talk out. We need to be honest with each other. That's what our huddle was built on!

Referee *blows the whistle.*

Referee:	*(To audience)* We have a delay of game on the offense. That's a five-yard penalty. It's STILL first down. *(To huddle)* You guys DO remember there's a clock in this game, don't you?
Player 1:	Of course we remember there's a clock, but that doesn't mean we have to be in a hurry.
Player 2:	Yeah, and a good huddle is hard to find. I'd been looking for a good huddle, and I'm thankful I finally found one.
Player 3:	We've gotten really close since we formed this huddle, and I just want you to know that these guys are very important to me.
Player 1:	You're important to us, too. Thanks for saying that.
Player 3:	Don't mention it! We're just glad to have you—glad to have all of you.
Player 4:	Yeah, I've been all over the world, and this huddle is the best thing I've ever been a part of. I just hope we can keep it together.
Referee:	If you don't do something—and do it fast—you're going to forfeit the game.
Player 2:	You know, this ref is getting really pushy! Why don't we all go get a drink of water and give him some time to calm down?
Player 1:	That's a great idea. Time out, Mr. Ref!
Referee:	*(To audience)* Time out!
Player 1:	Would you like to join us for something to drink?
Referee:	No thanks, I'll just stay here on the field and try to remember what game you're supposed to be playing.

Players *exit one way, and the* **Referee** *exits another. Lights down.*

THE END

READERS' THEATER

INTRO

In the Beginning Was the Word

At one time it was new and unique. Then it became old and boring. Now what once was lost has been found—the art of dramatic Scripture readings.

Do you remember the first time you saw a Scripture reading in church? You may have watched as several people stood at the front of the sanctuary with folders in hand—just reading. Occasionally they'd take turns…reading…words…in…a…sentence. Reading like the tick…tock…of…a… *(everybody together)* metronome. By the end of the reading, you…were…totally…asleep. That is, unless your best friend was sitting next to you, and you were both doing your best to not laugh out loud. Those readings always seemed like what churches would do if they couldn't pull off a real skit.

However, dramatic Scripture readings have made an impressive comeback! The key to doing a good Scripture reading is to look at the "big picture." What are you trying to accomplish? How can you make it more interesting than just listening to people read? Are you using people who can read the passage in an engaging and entertaining way? After all, the Bible is nothing less than the divine Word of God spoken to his disciples—and sometimes spoken by God himself. It deserves the utmost respect if you want it to have the utmost impact on listeners.

One of the greatest mistakes in putting together a Scripture reading is believing you can just choose a passage, pick some readers, and jump in without any practice. That's a recipe for a crummy, boring performance. A successful reading involves the right passage, divided the right way, and read by the right people. Done effectively, a good Scripture reading can bring a passage alive like nothing else can. (Unless you can get James Earl Jones to do the reading!)

Readers' Theater Top-10:

1. **Flex your cords.** It's a travesty when someone reads the Bible out loud and puts other people to sleep. We've all experienced a person killing the living Word by reading it in a monotone voice. So utilize inflection in your voice—realize that what you're reading is the greatest truth ever known to humanity. Don't overdo it as though you're reading a children's story; just make your reading as natural and energetic as possible.

2. **Don't be cold.** If you try to do a "cold reading" in front of an audience, you'll get a cold reception. Although readings can be easier to put together than actual skits, you still need to read through them several times in advance to get an idea of the appropriate tempo and flow of the piece. A few good rehearsals and read-throughs may even help develop more creative ideas for the readings. As you do those rehearsals, have the sound and lighting technicians (if you have them) sit in and watch. They may come up with some simple lighting or sound effects that could make your reading a home run.

3. **Don't stop, don't stop the music.** Some readings are very effective with nothing but silence behind them. However, using background music can give your reading more meaning and more emotion. Try to choose music that flows with the tempo of the reading. Also, an occasional Scripture reading can be an incredible addition to your worship time. The idea is to have a seamless transition from worship music into the reading and right back into singing. What a powerful moment it would be if your musician(s) could flow from backing up your reading and go straight into leading your group in worship.

4. **Leave the Cheese Whiz® at home.** Of all the different types of dramatic presentations in this book, Scripture readings are the easiest to "cheesify." Make sure your readers work hard to avoid the obvious cheese traps that lie waiting for them in the creative venue. For instance, no using a British accent. No moving the head like a beauty contestant reciting her plan to change the world. And, as always, avoid… talking…at…metronome…tempo!

5. **This is an "all skate" in verse direction.** If you're using presentation software (such as PowerPoint or MediaShout), then give the audience a chance to read with you. It will engage them more and help them relate to the reading if they're allowed to participate. Simply mark the Scripture you want them to recite in a way that will make it simple for them to follow along. The audience doesn't have to read the whole passage; just have them join in when appropriate between the actors' lines.

6. **Send out the outfit memo.** Sometimes uniformity can be a good thing. Show the audience you've got this together. Put them at ease with what you wear, as well as what you say and how you say it.

7. **Crank up the volume.** Have someone (a team member or the director) sit in the audience and listen to the voice levels. A lot of times there aren't enough microphones

for every reader, so have this person move around the church or auditorium as you read your lines. Can the audience hear you? If not, sadly, you're wasting your time. Be heard!

8. **What the world needs now is love.** You will be speaking on some heavy issues. You will be giving God's Word a voice. You will be looking into the eyes of the audience and see people looking down out of shame and guilt. You will also see people looking bored or uninterested or bitter. So you share with love. You share with conviction. You share with faith that you're making a difference as God ministers to hearts. For the brief moments while you're up there, you *are* the minister! So minister with love (it truly does cover a multitude of sins).

9. **Look at me when I'm talking to you!** When you practice on stage, keep the audience in mind—even with your eyes. Take note of when you have your lines memorized and look at the audience. If you're spending too much time reading with your head down, practice learning the lines so you can look at the audience more often. If there's no eye contact, then we (the audience) will be bored.

10. **Have fun.** Readers' theater offers freedom. You aren't blocking, memorizing a whole script, or having to go through hours and hours of rehearsal. If your team works on this Top-10 list and does the necessary disciplines, you'll have a great piece. And the fact that the audience gets to interact and read some lines makes it that much better. So let the audience see that you love what you do. Let the audience see your enthusiasm, and it will be infectious. It's a great responsibility to be onstage and carry out these messages, so do it justice…and have FUN!

"LOVE"

**BY RIAN SLAY, WITH REVISIONS BY TOMMY WOODARD
AND EDDIE JAMES**

WHAT: As demonstrated by this responsive reading, love is victorious.

WHO: Reader 1, Reader 2, Reader 3, Reader 4, All

WHEN: Present Day

WEAR: Depends on the drama team or group of actors: Some like to be uniformly
(COSTUMES dressed (all black, same pants and different colored shirts, etc.). Music stands
AND PROPS) could be used if actors want scripts in front of them.

WHY: 1 Corinthians 13

HOW: This script is very conducive to being read by non-actors along with the congregation. (Note: Let congregation know beforehand that they can join reading aloud where "All" is indicated.) Let the message of the words soak through the voice of each person who reads.

THEMES: Love, Pain, Trials, Trust, Faith, Hope

TIME: 4 minutes

Reader 1: Love is patient and kind.

Reader 2: Love is not jealous or boastful or proud or rude.

Reader 3: It does not demand its own way.

Reader 4: It is not irritable, and it keeps no record of being wronged.

Reader 1: It does not rejoice about injustice, but rejoices whenever the truth wins out.

Reader 2: Love never gives up, never loses faith.

Reader 3: It is always hopeful and endures through every circumstance.

All:	Love never gives up.
Reader 3:	So when you get that phone call, the one you've been dreading…
Reader 2:	So when your son turns to the bottle to deal with the pain…
Reader 1:	And when the best thing you can do for him is turn him away…
Reader 4:	And when the doctor looks at you and says, "It's cancer…"
Reader 2:	When the doctors are talking about time left and pain management…
Reader 1:	When the boss is talking about layoffs and cutbacks…
Reader 3:	When your whole world is turned upside down…
All:	Love never gives up.
Reader 2:	When your teenage daughter looks at you with tears in her eyes and says, "Dad, I'm pregnant…"
All:	Love never gives up.
Reader 1:	When you feel like there is a dark cloud hanging over your head that won't go away…
All:	Love never gives up.
Reader 4:	When they say you've lost your job…
All:	Love never gives up.
Reader 3:	When he walks away and never comes back…
All:	Love never gives up.
Reader 1:	Because when it seemed like all was lost, like their only hope was gone, and the world was dark…
Reader 3:	Love never gave up.
Reader 2:	When he hung on that cross with the weight of all my sin and shame on his shoulders…
Reader 4:	Love never gave up.

Reader 1:	When they put him in a tomb and rolled a stone over it to seal him in…
Reader 3:	Love never gave up.
Reader 1:	With guards posted
Reader 4:	And night falling
Reader 3:	And all hope seemed lost
Reader 2:	Love never gave up.
Reader 1:	Because when I was lost, blind, and alone…
Reader 3:	Love never gave up.
Reader 2:	When I had no way out and nowhere to go…
Reader 1, 2, 3, 4:	Love never gave up.
Reader 1:	When I was drowning in my own sin and shame…
Reader 2:	And the hurt and sins of my past wouldn't leave me alone…
Reader 1, 2, 3, 4:	Love never gave up.
Reader 1:	So when the doctor is searching for a reason for that cancer to be gone…
Reader 2:	And when your son calls and says, "Dad, I'm sorry. I need help."
Reader 3:	And when the sun begins to shine, and that dark cloud is lifted…
Reader 4:	When God provides in ways you never imagined…
Reader 1:	When you hold that precious baby in your arms…
All:	Love never gives up.
Reader 2:	Three things will last forever:
Reader 1:	Faith
Reader 3:	Hope

Reader 4:   And Love,

Reader 2:   And the greatest of these is:

All: Love.

THE END

"PSALM 13:6"
BY RIAN SLAY

WHAT: This script celebrates God because God is good!

WHO: Reader 1, Reader 2, Reader 3, All

WHEN: Present Day

WEAR: (COSTUMES AND PROPS) Depends on the drama team or group of actors: Some like to be uniformly dressed (all black, same pants and different colored shirts, etc.). Music stands could be used if actors want scripts in front of them.

WHY: Psalm 13:6

HOW: These lines should be presented in a real and honest way and with a sense of celebration. (Note: Let congregation know beforehand that they can join reading aloud where "All" is indicated.)

THEMES: Praise, Worship, Faith, Trust

TIME: 3 minutes

Reader 1: I will sing to the Lord because he is good to me.

Reader 2: I will SING!

Reader 3: I will sing to the Lord!

All: Because he is good.

Reader 1: Not because my life is perfect.

Reader 2: Because it's not.

All: Because he is good.

Reader 3: Not because I feel like it.

Reader 2:   Sometimes I just don't.

Reader 1, 2, 3:   I will sing to the Lord…

All: Because he is good.

Reader 1:   Not because I'm happy…

Reader 2:   Because life is tough.

Reader 3:   And sometimes I get sad.

Reader 1, 2, 3:   I will sing to the Lord…

All: Because he is good.

Reader 2:   Not because I'm succeeding.

Reader 1:   Sometimes I will fail.

Reader 3:   Not because I'm winning.

Reader 2:   Sometimes I will lose.

Reader 1, 2, 3:   I will sing to the Lord…

All: Because he is good.

Reader 1:   Not because I'm cool.

Reader 2:   Not because I'm popular or people like me.

Reader 1:   Because people are fickle and tomorrow they may not.

Reader 2:   Not because I've got it all together.

Reader 1:   Because tomorrow my world could fall apart.

Reader 3:   Not because things are going right.

Reader 2:   Though I'm grateful when they are.

Reader 1, 2, 3:   I will sing to the Lord…

All: Because he is good.

Reader 3:	He is good always.
Reader 1:	No matter what.
Reader 2:	He never changes.
Reader 1:	He is always good.
Reader 3:	So I will sing.
Reader 2:	I will sing loud!
Reader 1:	With all I've got!
Reader 2:	With all my heart!
Reader 3:	I will make a JOYFUL noise unto the Lord!
Reader 1, 2, 3:	I will sing to the Lord…
All:	Because he is good to me.

THE END

"PSALM 51"

BY SARAH VANDERAA

SKIT

6.3

WHAT: Echoing King David's confession, this script is an honest prayer to the God of mercy and forgiveness.

WHO: Speaker 1, Speaker 2, Speaker 3, Speaker 4

WHEN: Present Day

WEAR:
(COSTUMES AND PROPS) Depends on the drama team or group of actors: Some like to be uniformly dressed (all black, same pants and different colored shirts, etc.). Music stands could be used if actors want scripts in front of them.

WHY: Psalm 51

HOW: This piece consists of many short phrases to help bring out the meaning behind the words. While each word and phrase should be emphasized in a slower manner, each phrase that comes next should almost overlap with the one preceding it to help the listener find the connection more easily.

THEMES: Mercy, Grace, Forgiveness, Sin, Repentance

TIME: 5 minutes

Speaker 1: *(Begging)* Have mercy on me, O God.

Speaker 2: Mercy….grace…pity,

Speaker 3: *(Ashamed)* On me.

Speaker 4: *(Quietly honest)* The nastiest of sinners.

Speaker 2: *(Downcast)* I don't deserve mercy.

Speaker 3: I never have.

Speaker 4: According to your unfailing love.

Speaker 1:	*(Hopeful) Unfailing* love.
Speaker 3:	Constant.
Speaker 4:	Never-ending.
Speaker 2:	According to your great compassion, blot out…
Speaker 3:	Erase…
Speaker 2:	*(Pleading)* Wipe away my transgressions.
Speaker 1:	*(Owning the sin)* My sin.
Speaker 4:	*(Quiet)* Every unkind action.
Speaker 3:	*(More quiet)* Every lie.
Speaker 2:	*(Even quieter)* Every dirty look.
Speaker 1:	*(Whisper)* Everything.
Speaker 4:	*(Imploring, but not expecting)* Wash away all my iniquity,
Speaker 2:	And cleanse me from my sin.
Speaker 3:	My offenses and misdemeanors.
Speaker 1:	My bad behavior and failings.
Speaker 2:	*(Feeling guilty)* My sin is always before me.
Speaker 4:	*(Embarrassed)* Clear as day. Front and center.
Speaker 1:	*(Quietly sickened)* Against you, you only, have I sinned,
Speaker 3:	You…only you.
Speaker 4:	And done what is evil in your sight,
Speaker 2:	*(Understanding)* So that you are justified when you judge.
Speaker 1:	I messed up and deserve any punishment you give me.
Speaker 3:	*(Realizes the punishment deserved)* I deserve…death…hell. *(Slight pause)*

Speaker 2:	I was sinful at birth,
Speaker 3:	Right from the start.
Speaker 4:	*(Bleak)* Is it even possible for me to do anything right?
Speaker 1:	Ever?
Speaker 3:	You desire truth, and you teach me wisdom.
Speaker 2:	Which means...I *know* right from wrong,
Speaker 4:	But executing "right,"
Speaker 2:	*(Sincere)* That's when it gets tricky.
Speaker 4:	*(Softly insistent)* Cleanse me. Wash me.
Speaker 1:	And I will be whiter than snow.
Speaker 3:	More pure than water from a mountain spring.
Speaker 2:	*(Starting to gain hope)* Let me hear joy and gladness,
Speaker 4:	May the bones you have crushed rejoice.
Speaker 3:	*(Beginnings of excitement)* Celebrate!
Speaker 1:	Hide your face from my sins,
Speaker 2:	My sins.
Speaker 3:	*(Openly admit)* Mine.
Speaker 4:	*(Prayerful, hopeful)* Create in me,
Speaker 2:	*(Show deep desire)* A pure heart,
Speaker 3:	Unpolluted.
Speaker 1:	And renew a steadfast spirit within me.
Speaker 3:	Unwavering.
Speaker 4:	Do not cast me,

Speaker 3:	*(Scared at idea)* Unwanted.
Speaker 2:	From your presence,
Speaker 4:	*(Joyful expression)* Restore to me the joy of your salvation,
Speaker 1:	And grant me a willing spirit to sustain me…
Speaker 3:	*(Show readiness)* A ready spirit.
Speaker 2:	*(Display eagerness)* An eager spirit.
Speaker 4:	My tongue will sing of your righteousness.
Speaker 3:	*(Joyful)* Sing!
Speaker 2:	With a full heart,
Speaker 1:	And open hands.
Speaker 3:	*(Louder than before)* Sing!
Speaker 2:	*(Louder than before)* With a full heart,
Speaker 1:	*(Louder than before)* And open hands.
Speaker 4:	O Lord, open my lips,
Speaker 2:	And my mouth will declare your praise.
Speaker 3:	Only your praise,
Speaker 4:	The sacrifices of God are a broken spirit;
Speaker 1:	*(Humbled)* Broken.
Speaker 3:	Fixed only through your forgiveness.
Speaker 2:	*(Quietly expectant, truly sorry)* Forgive me, *(Pause)* please.
Speaker 4:	As only you can.
Speaker 1:	Forgive.
Speaker 2:	Me.

Speaker 3:   A sinner.

Speaker 4:   Amen.

THE END

"NOT ENOUGH"

BY SARAH VANDERAA, WITH REVISIONS BY TOMMY WOODARD
AND EDDIE JAMES

WHAT: What do you do with your dreams when harsh words linger in your heart?

WHO: Man 1, Woman 1, Man 2, Woman 2; *Optional:* Child, Middle School Girl, Coach, Boyfriend, Boss, Doctor, Publisher, Parent, Narrator

WHEN: Present Day

WEAR: Depends on the drama team or group of actors: Some like to be uniformly dressed (all black, same pants and different colored shirts, etc.). Music stands could be used if actors want scripts in front of them.
(COSTUMES AND PROPS)

WHY: Psalm 139:1-16; John 3:16

HOW: The four characters in this script can be read by either teens or adults with equal effectiveness, as long as they thoroughly absorb the lines.

THEMES: Rejection, Lies, Truth, Bitterness, Dreams, Acceptance

TIME: 7 minutes

Man 1:	Rejection.
Woman 1:	*(Accepting)* It's part of life.
Man 2:	So much so, we assume it's the part of life we just have to live with and can't get rid of...ever.
Woman 2:	People say it's a natural part of life.
Man 1:	That's really just a good excuse.
Man 2:	It's a way to try to cover the pain.
Woman 1:	Or to pretend it doesn't hurt.

Woman 2:	*(Honestly)* But it does. It really does.
Man 1:	No one likes to hear they aren't good enough.
Woman 1:	Pretty enough.
Man 2:	Strong enough.
Woman 2:	Talented enough.
Man 1:	And rejection isn't biased to age.
Woman 1:	It starts when we are very young.

NOTE TO DIRECTOR: *For the next several lines, another group of other actors can say them, or you can give one line to each* **READER** *to say. Your stage may become crowded with additional actors, so it might be easier just to give these lines to the* **READERS** *and have them portray each of these feelings.*

Child:	*(Snubs)* You can't play on our team because you don't know how to play soccer.
Middle School Girl:	*(Snobbish)* My mom let me invite only 10 girls to my birthday party, and you would have made 11. Sorry.
Coach:	I had to cut someone from the team, and you just aren't varsity basketball material.
Boyfriend:	*(Brushes off)* I liked dating you, but I found someone else…
Boss:	We had to make cutbacks, and you were the newest member on staff…
Publisher:	*Dear Mr. Anderson, we regret to inform you that at this time we cannot publish your book…*
Doctor:	Your cancer is too advanced. We cannot accept you into the clinical trials…
Parent:	You never do anything right! Just once I wish I could be proud of my own kid…

Back to the original **Readers**…

Woman 1:	And so we become bitter.

Man 2:	We become hardened.
Woman 2:	Our dreams gather dust and slowly die.
Man 1:	We accept our realities and lose our passion for life.
Woman 1:	For anything worth fighting for.
Woman 2:	We believe the lie that rejection is our fate.
Man 1:	We accept that we are nothing special.
Woman 1:	We follow the crowd.
Man 2:	Doing our best to blend in with the rest of faceless humanity.
Woman 2:	Once in a while, we'll be reminded of our dreams.
Man 1:	And something will momentarily spark in us.
Woman 1:	But all the previous rejection comes rushing back, stamping down desire for anything more.
Man 2:	So we stay under the radar.
Man 1:	Making sure we live normal enough lives that keep the attention away from us.
Woman 2:	Keep *(Emphasize)* **rejection** away from us.
Woman 1:	Because to be great…you will be rejected.
Man 2:	Rejection simply confirms what you've always guessed…
Man 1:	What you've always known.
Woman 2:	That you are unlovable.
Woman 1:	That you are unsuccessful.
Man 1:	That you will never add up.
Man 2:	That your talents are mediocre.
Woman 2:	It feels like a knife in your heart.

Woman 1:   And each rejection pushes it in a little further, twists it a little more.

Man 2:   The ache is deep and always there.

Woman 2:   A constant reminder.

Man 1:   Sometimes it seems like rejection is this massive black hole, and you can't stop falling.

Man 2:   When all that you want, what you've always wanted, is just to feel accepted.

Woman 1:   Special.

Man 1:   Loved.

Man 2:   Why can't there be someone like that?

Woman 2:   Someone who loves and even *likes* you, no matter what?

Man 1:   Someone who thinks you're the most special person who ever lived?

Woman 1:   Someone who would give his life for you—believing your life is worth that much?

Man 1:   Someone like that...I'd follow anywhere.

Narrator: "For God so loved the world that he gave his one and only Son, that whoever believes in him shall not perish but have eternal life." (John 3:16)

Man 1:   Oh Lord, you have searched me and you know me.

Woman 1:   You know when I sit and when I rise; you perceive my thoughts from afar.

Man 2:   You discern my going out and my lying down;

Woman 2:   You are familiar with all my ways.

Man 2:   Before a word is on my tongue, you know it completely, oh Lord.

Woman 1:   You hem me in—

Woman 2:   Behind and before;

Man 1:	You have laid your hand upon me.
Man 2:	Such knowledge is too wonderful for me,
Woman 2:	Too lofty for me to attain.
Woman 1:	Where can I go from your Spirit?
Woman 2:	Where can I flee from your presence?
Man 1:	If I go up to the heavens,
Woman 1:	You are there;
Man 2:	If I make my bed in the depths,
Woman 1:	You are there.
Man 2:	If I rise on the wings of the dawn, if I settle on the far side of the sea,
Woman 2:	Even there your hand will guide me,
Man 1:	Your right hand will hold me fast.
Woman 1:	If I say, "Surely the darkness will hide me and the light become night around me,"
Man 1:	Even the darkness will not be dark to you;
Man 2:	The night will shine like the day, for darkness is as light to you.
Man 1:	For you created my inmost being;
Woman 2:	You knit me together in my mother's womb.
Woman 1:	I praise you because I am fearfully
Man 1:	And wonderfully
Man 2:	Made;
Man 1:	Your works are wonderful,
Woman 2:	I know that full well.

Woman 1:	My frame was not hidden from you when I was made in the secret place.
Man 1:	When I was woven together in the depths of the earth,
Woman 2:	Your eyes saw my unformed body.
Man 2:	All the days ordained for me were written in your book before one of them came to be. (Psalm 139:1-16)

THE END

SKIT
6.5

"WHERE'S GOD?"

BY SARAH VANDERAA, WITH REVISIONS BY TOMMY WOODARD AND EDDIE JAMES

WHAT: Asks the question, "Where is God in the hard times?"

WHO: Narrator (teen or adult), Woman, Teen Guy, Man

WHEN: Present Day

WEAR: (COSTUMES AND PROPS) Depends on the drama team or group of actors: Some like to be uniformly dressed (all black, same pants and different colored shirts, etc.). Music stands could be used if actors want scripts in front of them.

WHY: Psalm 22:1-2; 69:1-3

HOW: This Readers' Theater expresses pain and anguish. Many raw feelings are within this piece. Really work on it. When you feel like you have it down, work on it some more. Be sure the readers don't just "read" these lines but are in the moment as they recite them. Make sure you have someone pointing out "melodramatic" moments so you can avoid them; you want "real" moments. At the end when you offer the HOPE, make sure the readers look at the audience and make eye contact with people—as if talking just to them.

THEMES: Anger, Bitterness, God's Silence, Desperation

TIME: 5 minutes

Narrator: My God, my God, why have you forsaken me? Why are you so far from saving me, so far from my cries of anguish? My God, I cry out by day, but you do not answer, by night, but I find no rest. (Psalm 22:1-2)

Woman: *(Quiet)* Silence, dead silence.

(Pause)

Teen Guy: Nothing, no answer.

(Pause)

Man: Only darkness, *eternal* darkness.

(Pause)

Woman: Is this what hell is like? No answer?

Man: God is so distant. I'm not sure God really exists.

Teen Guy: *(Cynical)* God, what God? There is no God.

Woman: I gave up on God a long time ago.

Man: Why? Well, it's rather simple, really.

Teen Guy: *(Matter-of-fact)* God gave up on me. You know how I know? I never got any answers to the questions I was asking.

Woman: *(Frustrated confusion)* All I ever got was a jumble of overpowering emotions and thoughts that kept rotating around my mind...never leaving...never giving me a moment's peace.

Man: Along with a dead silence from God.

Teen Guy: Nothing.

Woman: You want proof?

Teen Guy: I have lots of proof.

Man: The story goes like this...

Woman: I traveled to India for a job conference two years ago. Poverty was everywhere— *(Sardonic)* except in the five-star hotel where I was staying. While taking a tour, I saw overwhelming poverty. *(Quiet despair)* Not being a citizen, there wasn't much I could do. And I felt a deep sadness...and rage. At myself for my wealth. At the government for letting this happen. And at God for seeming absent from this land.

Teen Guy: God's absent in my house. My dad is the proof. My dad *(Pause, acceptance, almost factual)* has been a drunk for most of his life. *(Rapidly move through the next sentence with increasing intensity and anger)* And when he gets drunk, he gets angry, and when he gets angry...

	(Pause for breath) it's never a pretty sight. I have to protect my mom from his beatings—taking most of it myself. *(Hurt, untrusting)* I hate him. I hate myself for not reporting him. I hate God for leaving me to defend myself.
Man:	*(Angry, frustrated, at the end of his rope)* I hate him. My boss is constantly berating me, demanding more work and longer hours, while I stay at the same pay grade. He refuses to listen to my ideas; and I'm frustrated, angry, and ready to quit. But the economy is in the toilet, and I won't get another job. I've tried, but I can't find anything. So I'm trapped. And God? No help from God.
Woman:	*(Cold, indifferent)* I began to depend heavily on over-the-counter drugs.
Teen Guy:	*(Apathetic)* I began cutting.
Man:	*(Listless)* I began drinking.
Woman:	It seemed logical.
Teen Guy:	It seemed like the only way to escape the pain.
Man:	*(Blunt, fuming)* So excuse me if I'm not quite into God right now.
Woman:	*(Outspoken, irate)* God deserted the poor.
Teen Guy:	My family.
Man:	*(Forthright, seething)* ME!
Teen Guy:	*(Direct, livid)* God put people in my life that I… *(Pause, whisper)* trusted.
Man:	*(Quieter, still angry)* My boss.
Woman:	The government.
Teen Guy:	My dad.
Woman:	But they let me down.
Man:	And when I needed God the most, God took off.
Teen Boy:	And left me to deal with the mess.

Woman:	*(Incredulous)* So why would I trust God?
Man:	*(Disbelief)* Trust God?
Teen Guy:	What a joke!
Woman:	I won't be a fool again.
Man:	Because there is silence, only silence.

(Pause)

Narrator:	Save me, O God, for the waters have come up to my neck. I sink in the miry depths, where there is no foothold. I have come into the deep waters; the floods engulf me. I am worn out calling for help; my throat is parched. (Psalm 69:1-3) To some, silence is deafening. But to God, it's a chance to talk, to speak into the deepest places of our hearts. It's a chance for God to teach us that he doesn't always make himself known through earthquakes or thunderstorms. No, sometimes God comes to us in the silence, the stillness. And it's in the silence of our darkest times that we must open our hearts and minds to hear the voice of God.
Woman:	You may find yourself feeling these same emotions. You may feel as though God has left the building.
Man:	Life, in many ways, can hurt. You may be hurting. Can we gently remind you of the Father's embrace? You may feel and even see the miry depths.
Teen Guy:	You may find no foothold, only deep waters. Don't give up! God is still God! God knows your hurt. God knows your pain.
Narrator:	Call out to God even if your throat is parched. God is the Living Water. God hears our cries.

THE END

Skits That Teach

Lactose Free for Those Who Can't Stand Cheesy Skits

Eddie James and Tommy Woodard

35 CHEESE-FREE SKITS

If you're looking for fun and creative ways to involve your students in learning, you can stop looking. *Skits That Teach* provides you and your students everything you need to act out funny and compelling skits with total confidence.

Search by topic or by group size to find the perfect comedic or dramatic sketch to help illustrate a point or just start a dialogue. The Skit Guys, Eddie James and Tommy Woodard, have tested these skits on teenagers around the country, and they've brought together some of the best for this great resource. Plus they give you everything you need for each skit—overview, characters, location, Scripture reference, props, direction pointers, and a complete script.

The Skit Guys avoid the cheesy dialogues and scenes typically found in Christian dramas and instead bring fun characters, witty scripts, and entertaining situations to their skits, all categorized by:

- Skits for Idiots (it would take an idiot not to be able to do them right!)
- Monologues
- Duets/Ensembles
- Comedy
- Drama
- Scripture Readings

Available in stores and online!

We Illustrate, You Teach.

On each volume:
7 movies
7 study guides
7 teaching outlines
7 small group questions

Available at skitguys.com and wherever books are sold.

Need a drama team?
Need to train your actors?
Need directing tips?
Need to know how to write a good script?
Need methods for memorizing lines?
Need to learn how to do improv?

- - - - - - - - - - - ▶ Need it ALL on one DVD?

LET **THE SKIT GUYS** SHOW YOU HOW

SKIT
TRAINING
101

DRAMA
COACH
IN A BOX

How many solutions do we have to your script needs?

Hundreds.

Share Your Thoughts

With the Author: Your comments will be forwarded to
the author when you send them to *zauthor@zondervan.com*.

With Zondervan: Submit your review of this book
by writing to *zreview@zondervan.com*.

Free Online Resources at

www.zondervan.com

Zondervan AuthorTracker: Be notified whenever your favorite
authors publish new books, go on tour, or post an update
about what's happening in their lives at www.zondervan.com/
authortracker.

Daily Bible Verses and Devotions: Enrich your life with daily
Bible verses or devotions that help you start every morning
focused on God. Visit www.zondervan.com/newsletters.

Free Email Publications: Sign up for newsletters on Christian
living, academic resources, church ministry, fiction, children's
resources, and more. Visit www.zondervan.com/newsletters.

Zondervan Bible Search: Find and compare Bible passages in
a variety of translations at www.zondervanbiblesearch.com.

Other Benefits: Register yourself to receive online benefits
like coupons and special offers, or to participate in research.

ZONDERVAN®

ZONDERVAN.com/
AUTHORTRACKER
follow your favorite authors